ACKNOWLEDGEMENTS

I would like to thank all my friends, both within and outside network marketing, who have helped to make this book possible. You're the best!

© John Bremner 1994, 1996

The right of John Bremner to be identified as the author of this work has been asserted by him in accordance with the Copyright, Designs and Patents Act 1988.

First published in 1994, as *How To Make Your Fortune Through Network Marketing*, by Judy Piatkus (Publishers) Ltd of 5 Windmill Street, London W1P 1HF

First published as *Professional Network Marketing* in 1996

A catalogue record for this book is available from the British Library

ISBN 0 7499 1625 7

Edited by Carol Franklin
Designed by Paul Saunders

Typeset and revised by
Phoenix Photosetting, Chatham, Kent
Printed and bound in Great Britain by
Biddles Ltd, Guildford & King's Lynn

PROFESSIONAL
NETWORK
MARKETING

JOHN BREMNER

PROFESSIONAL
NETWORK
MARKETING

Practical Advice
for Building a
Successful Network

PIATKUS

CONTENTS

INTRODUCTION

Many thousands of millionaires in the USA have made their fortune through multi-level or network marketing. Hundreds of thousands of ordinary people make a very good living from it. Now, throughout the world, network marketing is beginning to take an increasingly important place as the most flexible, affordable, and viable new business for those who choose to earn extra money through their own efforts. It has all the benefits of a franchise without the cost.

People from every walk of life are being tempted into network marketing by the promise of unlimited earnings potential. It is the only business opportunity available where your background doesn't matter in the least. It is not what you have been that matters, it is what you will do now. Some of the laziest layabouts in recent history have been galvanised into action by the promise of riches ahead for those who will do what it takes.

This is the promise that network marketing makes to each and every new distributor:

'Do what it takes to operate our business successfully and you can become rich beyond your wildest dreams and have as much free time as you would like to spend your money in.'

It sounds like a wild claim, doesn't it? Of course, most people who join don't become millionaires. In fact, most people who join don't stay around long enough to find out if they could have made it in the business. They quit at the first sign of failure. They may have shown their product to some friends and got an adverse reaction or they may have tried to introduce some new distributors to the business and been disappointed when they failed to sign up. Whatever the reasons, the fact is that when the product is at all difficult to sell and success is slow, about 80 per cent of new dealers drop out or fade away within their first six months.

We are not really interested in the failures. The purpose of this book is to point you in the right direction so that you will be one of the 20 per cent who don't quit and go on to be one of the success statistics of network marketing.

Do you want to be one of the top money earners in the world? Read on.

One of John Paul Getty's most famous sayings is 'I'd rather earn 1 per cent of a hundred people's efforts than 100 per cent of my own.' In one sentence, that is the principle behind network marketing.

When you 'sign on' with a network marketing company you are effectively licensed in two areas – to trade in the company's products and to recruit new distributors like yourself. Each of these new distributors then does the same and recruits new distributors of their own. Thus your group grows and your network spreads. This process is called sponsoring and, if you sponsor successfully, there is absolutely no limit to the number of distributors that you can have in your group. How you benefit from this is that since you get 1 or 2 per cent of the turnover of all of them, down to five generations in the best companies, there is absolutely no limit to your potential earnings – as a hundred thousand American millionaires will testify.

There are a number of different profit centres available for the distributors of a network marketing company, from the straightforward retailing of the product as a dealer or distributor to the management of a huge international business with a network of thousands of distributors in your organisation.

This book is aimed at helping you reach whatever level you feel comfortable at. If you only want to be a small-scale distributor, earning a bit of extra cash to pay for that holiday or car by retailing a few of your chosen company's unique products on a regular basis, then you will find enough information in this book to help you do just that very effectively. If, on the other hand, you want to go as far as you can go in your chosen network marketing organisation, then you will find everything you need to know to achieve that aim within these covers.

For those who are new to the business and impatient to get started, turn now to the Nutshell Guide which follows this introduction. You can then work through the rest of this book as you learn the business.

For those who like to have real in-depth knowledge before they start something – read on, but please bear one thing in mind as you read. Network marketing is a simple business. All you really need to do is to sell the product and introduce some friends. Keep on doing that and you can make as much money as you can spend.

No matter what business you are involved with, the moment you stop learning, you start fading. It is not enough simply to read this book. You have to put the principles into practice. If you work through this book instead of just reading it, you will learn a lot more about yourself and your potential. You will not only increase your effectiveness in sales, but also in business and as a person.

You may get lucky if you happen to sign on with the right company at the right time and end up making a fortune without having to expend much effort, but that is not the way it usually works. The rewards you receive are more often directly related to the effort that you put in. Even so, that is still such more than you can say for most other businesses.

At the end of each chapter you will find space for notes. Whenever you read something that triggers your interest or sparks off a new idea of your own, write it down before you forget it. Extract the information that you find most useful for your own situation and write that down too. By the end of the book you will have a unique core of facts, ideas, tips and mind triggers. Remember that one really good idea can make you a fortune. The most successful distributors are thinkers, doers and true innovators. They are full of ideas which they put to good use every day. Don't let *your* ideas go to waste.

Only 20 per cent of readers will really put this book to good use. If it becomes so beaten up that you have to tape it together, then you are using it properly.

It's up to you now.

In a Nutshell

So, you have taken this book into your hands, glanced through the contents and thought *'Whew! You mean I have to do all this?'*

No, you don't have to do it all! At least not straight away. To get started immediately, begin here with this Nutshell Guide. You will then have a good general idea of what network marketing is all about, and of how you fit in and what to do. You can read the rest of the book as you are learning the trade. The important thing is to get out there and *do it*. Start selling your company's product. Start earning yourself some real money. Start being a winner. Get up out of your chair and sell. It's where the money is.

First things first. Decide what you want from life. Write down what you want and never forget it. It will help motivate you and keep you going when things get tough.

Be sure to keep your eyes wide open though. There are a lot of network marketing companies out there, and some of them last weeks rather than years, and make their money by preying on the gullible.

Be very aware of the brainwashing techniques used by certain of the less scrupulous companies. Beginners can easily get caught up in the excitement of a well-planned Business Briefing and may end up investing far more than they can comfortably afford. If you approach or are approached by a company or a sponsor, a number of simple precautions can protect you against deception.

1. Carefully check the background of the company in which you are interested before you jump in with both feet, thus at least ensuring that the company is successful, and will be around long enough to pay your commissions and bonuses. If you know who their suppliers are, then ask these companies for a credit reference. Don't put your confidence in a company that does not pay its bills promptly. (See Chapter 2).

2. If high income claims are made by individuals who are trying to get you to part with cash, make sure that you see their latest company cheque – and remember that not all this may be profit. A £4,000 monthly cheque may seem impressive, but if £3,200 of this has to be paid out in 'downline rebates' (rebates to personally recruited members who have ordered stock), and overheads such as telephone and travel costs, not much profit is left for a month's work.

3. Remember that even the best companies will tend to understate their failures and overstate their successes. Be sceptical until you have satisfied yourself that the business is truly workable, but don't be so sceptical that you allow a great business opportunity to pass you by. There comes a time when you have to make up your mind. As a rough guide, you should be able to thoroughly check out a company, its product lines and business viability within four weeks maximum.

4. Don't be too greedy. Any company that promises you an overnight fortune for a heavy initial investment needs to be looked at through a microscope. It is far better to get involved with a reputable company and steadily build up your business from a modest beginning.

Once you have decided on your company, your initial investment and made your commitment by signing up and ordering stock, make out a list of all your friends, relatives and business associates. This list will become your *warm market*. These are the people you apporoach first. But, remember, a little knowledge can be dangerous. Whatever you do, don't go running round all of them full of enthusiasm before you know what you are talking about. This is known in the trade as '*burning them off*' and a lot of otherwise very sensible people have burned off their very best prospects by approaching them too soon.

Before you start visiting your warm market, there are a few things you need to do. Start by smartening up your appearance to make yourself look more businesslike and to gain a boost in your personal confidence.

The next thing you need to do before you start is learn how to sell. You may be one of the few natural salespersons around, but they are few and far between.

You can learn how to sell at company trainings, and by getting out into the field and actually doing it. Go with your 'sponsor' (the person who introduced you to the company) on your first few sales calls until you get the hang of it and, no matter what happens, never be put off. To become a successful salesperson you have to learn to accept the word 'no' on some occasions, because no matter how good the product and no matter how good you are at selling it, you will get your share of definite noes. Don't let them bother you. The warm glow that comes when you *do* sell makes it all worth while.

IN BRIEF

- **Decide what you want from life and write it down**
- **Choose your company carefully**
- **Sign up and order your stock**
- **Start selling**
- **Keep selling**

For a greater depth of knowledge: *enquire within*!

NOTES, IDEAS AND THINGS TO DO

– I –

AIMING FOR SUCCESS

Network marketing can give you anything you want from life. If what you want is simply an extra £50 a week to pay for that car or holiday, then that option is available to you in this business. If, on the other hand, you want a total change of lifestyle and riches that most people can only dream of, then that option is also available to you. Thus before you start there are two things that you have to decide. The first is, *what do you want from your life?*

This is the single, most important question that you will ever be asked. The answer could determine the entire course of your life.

Put your aims in writing

Make out a written list of everything that you want from life. The reason for this is simple. If you have a list you can refer to it and keep your aims in focus. You can check your progress, adjusting your aims up or down as necessary, congratulating yourself when you achieve an aim and motivating yourself to do what it takes to achieve the others.

If you fail to make a written list, you will only have a vague idea of what your aims are and will therefore only work towards them in a vague way.

Can you imagine the score you would achieve in a game of darts if you weren't aiming? Or do you know where you would end up if you got on a bus without looking at the destination? The same will happen with your life if you don't write down your aims list.

Now put this book down and write down a list of all your aims.

Be specific. If you want a car then don't just write down: 'A new car'. Write down the make, model, year, colour, engine capacity and trim level. If you want money in the bank, then write down how much you want.

The second question to ask is, *when do you want these things by?*

The time-scale is a very important factor in aim setting. You have to be realistic but ambitious. It is no use wanting everything by tomorrow, because that clearly won't happen, but on the other hand you don't want to have to wait too long for some things.

Of course, material things are of great importance to your long-term comfort and satisfaction, but don't forget the more elusive aims of personal development. One of the great things about network marketing is that you can grow personally with the business. When you start your business you may lack confidence. That will come with success, as will heightened self-esteem, leadership qualities and an outgoing personality. Look at the leaders of any industry and those are the qualities you will find. They needed those qualities to get the job. In network marketing you can start without them and develop them as you go along. I've seen it happen time and time again. I've seen everyone from shy housewives to semi-literate deep-sea fishermen grow into enthusiastic team motivators who can get up and speak for half an hour without scripts and leave their audience buzzing.

Go for the ceiling

One of the worst mistakes that you can make is setting your aims too low. If you watch an arrow in flight you will see that it travels in a parabola. If the archer fired it parallel with the ground then it would fall short of the target. The action of gravity will pull it down. Likewise, there is a gravity in force in our business that always tends to pull us up short of our target. You have to aim higher than your ambitions dictate.

If you have a bad self-image, you may be used to failure and will not want to set yourself high aims in case you don't achieve them. If you do this then you will find that you are making a self-fulfilling prophecy.

Make your long-term aims really ambitious. What are your dreams? What would you really like? Aim for the sky, not half-way up the hill!

Classify your aims into short term, medium term and long term. The only qualifications are that they must be possible. For example:

> *'I want to learn how to pilot a plane'* is a possible aim.
>
> *'I want to learn how to fly like Superman'* is an impossible aim.

Think about it. Have you lost dreams? Have you failed in the past to reach high enough? Have you let opportunities slip past you? If things haven't worked out for you in the past, now is the time to change all that.

Your only limit is your own imagination. If you can conceive it, then you can achieve it.

Here are a few examples of the sort of things you could aim for which I have borrowed from an extremely successful distributor. (At the time of writing he has achieved most of his initial list of medium-term aims and is now working on his long-term aims.) But remember, these are his. If you agree with any, adopt them, but in the main you will be choosing your own list.

Short-term aims	Time-scale
Stop drinking	Now
Write that letter I've been putting off	Now
Be more patient with others	Now
Think positively	Now
Stop smoking	Now
Get the car repaired	1 month
Pay off my overdraft	3 months
Buy a new music centre	3 months
Lose 4 in from my waistline	4 months
Build a local network of 16 distributors	4 months
Finish my home extension	6 months
Take a camping holiday by the sea	this summer

Medium-term aims	**Time-scale 1 year**

Own a new black BMW 535i with tan leather interior, factory-fitted CD player portable Cellnet telephone and alloy wheels

Become a totally confident and relaxed public speaker, and a brilliant and innovative trainer

Develop an unshakeable persistence and strength of character

Buy a four-bedroomed house in Devon, with a breathtaking view of the sea, full air conditioning, triple glazing and patio doors leading into a spacious garden

Write that novel that I've always been promising myself to write

Learn to speak fluent French and German

Support my favourite charity with 10 per cent of my income

Help my children achieve a good standard of education

Build a network of 500 distributors throughout the country

Take a month-long holiday in the Caribbean with my wife

Long-term aims	**Time-scale 5 years**

Build a huge international network of distributors

Become totally financially independent with £15,000,000 in the bank

Own luxury homes throughout the world

Gain the respect and friendship of everyone who comes into contact with me

Pilot my own private Citation jet aircraft and Robinson R22 helicopter

Go back to college and gain an Honours degree in psychology

Own an original Picasso

Achieve total peace of mind with a clear conscience

Enjoy this wonderful life!

Ambitious? You bet it is! Ambition is your guideline. Now go ahead and let your imagination build you the life you've always wanted. Remember, personal development is just as important to your long-term happiness as material wealth. It may even be that you cannot have one without the other.

Don't read any further until you have written your own aims down. If you ignore this part, you are cheating yourself out of your potential.

Now that you have your aims written down, don't just put them into a drawer and forget about them. Instead, work out how you are going to achieve them and then do what it takes to achieve them. Write down your aims neatly on a folding card and carry them with you at all times. If you feel yourself getting side-tracked or losing focus, pull out your card and study your aims. Everyone needs occasional reminders to pull their minds back into focus. It certainly works for me.

Self-motivation is the key to success in this business. 'Do it now!' should be your driving force. If you want a new car you won't earn it sitting in your old one.

Revising your aims

There may come a time when you realise that a certain aim was unrealistic in time-scale, either because you have already achieved it or because your realise that it will take a lot longer than you originally thought. Or there may be some other reason for your revision. You must accept that your best-laid plans may not always work out as you imagined. From the moment you start in network marketing your aims will be in a continual state of development – being updated, revised and constantly tested against reality. I have found that every situation has an upside and a downside. Don't dwell on the downside, instead – explore every possible aspect of the upside. You may be surprised how many advantages you can find in even the most difficult situation. Be like the legendary Buddhist who gazes out of his window in the early evening with a contented smile: 'I can see the setting sun, now that my barn has burned down,' he says. That is how optimistic *your* outlook should be.

Persistence towards your aims

The development of a greater level of persistence should be an aim in its own right. Instead of saying, 'I will try to make a success of network marketing', it is far better to say, 'I will persist at network marketing until I am successful, no matter how long it takes'.

'No matter how long it takes'! So what if you achieve nothing in your first year? Persist. So what if your group collapses a dozen times and you have to start all over again? Persist. So what if you can't find anyone who will work as hard as you? Persist. So what if it takes you ten years to build a successful organisation? Persist.

The long-term potential – the incredible long-term potential that can put your income on a par with industry leaders and show-business superstars – makes your success worth waiting for. It won't necessarily take ten years. It is possible to achieve that level of success in two to three years, but no matter how long it takes you must persist.

Remember the words of Edmund Burke: 'He who wrestles with us sharpens our skill, our antagonist is our helper.'

Each knock that you take and survive will toughen you and make you stronger. The school of hard knocks can be the best school there is. Commit to this business for as long as it takes to make enough money to retire on. After that you can relax. I believe that you would be foolish to give it up even then. I just can't think of anything else in the world that gives me so much fun. Anything I can do in public that is!

I am going to repeat a phrase that appears elsewhere in this book because I firmly believe it is the most important statement you will read within these covers: 'Until you have decided that you will never give up, you haven't given network marketing enough commitment to succeed.'

Persistence is the one personality trait that all successful people share. All the failures I have ever known in network marketing all lacked in this one essential area.

Visualisation

It's been called dyna/psyc, self-hypnosis and auto-suggestion. Joe Geraghty, a brilliant network marketing trainer with a psychology-slanted approach, calls it 'outcoming' and that name just about sums up the method.

You have to see the outcome of successfully achieving your aims. If you want to pay off that overdraft, then you have to visualise the whole thing. See yourself filling in the deposit form. See yourself counting the money out note by note. See yourself handing it over to the teller with a smile on your face. Hear his or her voice saying thank you. See yourself leaping for joy when you get out of the bank and no one is watching you. See your wife or husband kissing you, congratulating you.

Can you see all that?

If you can, nothing can stop you from achieving it. If you can't see it then practise until you can.

Get the picture?

Carry a picture of the material things that you desire. Get a picture of the car that you want. Use a small photo album to hold them conveniently. If you want a private plane then go to an airport and take a photo of the exact model. If you can get to sit in one then all the better. Strap yourself in. Drink in the feeling. Hold the joystick. Start up the plane if you can. Even better, arrange flying lessons. Think about it. Would that help your visualisation? You'd better believe it. If you can see it then you can do it. You could obtain your private pilot's licence for little more than the cost of an average family holiday.

Write to the manufacturer for the literature on the plane of your dreams. Feel the excitement and anticipation. Start saving for it right now, even if all you can manage is £1 a week. As your income improves through network marketing, you will be able to direct more towards your aim. The positive act of saving with a definite end in mind will start a chain of events that will bring that object of desire to you, without fail. The only question is how long it will take you. I know that this works from experience. Do it and so will you. If you really believe that you can get it, then nothing is beyond your reach.

You are the master of your own destiny. When you combine a deep belief in your own abilities with a deep desire, that is when the magic begins. Let's say that you *do* want a private plane. We will accept that this could be quite a difficult aim to achieve for the average person, so how is it that many fairly average individuals own their own plane?

● The answer is simple – they wanted to own one!

● The question is equally simple – how badly do you want to own one?

● If you say, 'I'd quite like one' – that is not good enough.

- If you say, 'I'd really like one' – that is still not good enough.

- If you say, 'I want one more than anything on earth and I'm going to do what it takes to get it, no matter how long it takes me!' – then you are on your way to becoming the owner of your own private plane.

Albert Einstein, the philosopher scientist, said that if any man can concentrate for three minutes then he can conquer the world.

Einstein was a very wise man. He knew that pure concentration, even for three minutes, is difficult to achieve. Time yourself and find out. Can you really concentrate without stray thoughts butting in?

Well, it's hard to achieve, but it can be done. The other thing Einstein was saying was that hardly any of us exploit our full potential. He was a man who hated to see lives going to waste. Don't let it happen to you! Use every precious minute to its fullest advantage.

Stay focused on your aims until, one by one, you achieve them. One by one! Remember that. When you have decided what is your next aim, don't get sidetracked half-way through and decide to go for something else. Only by fixed concentration can your aims be achieved. This does not just apply to your aims in network marketing, but to all the aims in your life. Half-hearted attempts never win.

It is important to remember that simply wanting something won't bring it to you unless you do what it takes to get what you want. What do *you* have to do? Work longer hours? Give up drinking? Move to a smaller house to release capital? Move to where the work is? Work harder than you've ever worked in your life? Give up TV? Give up your steady job to allow more time for networking? Get up earlier in the morning? Improve your business education? Whatever you have to do – do it!

Practise your visualisation at least four times every day. Try to get some time alone, and pull out your photos and your aims list. Start by taking a deep breath and letting it out slowly. Close your eyes and take another deep breath, then let it out slowly. Allow yourself to relax totally. Work your way through your body, one muscle group at a time, until you have no tense muscles. Treat your mind in the same way. Get rid of all those intrusive, irrelevant thoughts – they disturb true concentration.

Now carefully read through your aims. Have you achieved any of them today? Are you doing what it takes? Feel yourself flying that plane. See yourself standing in front of a huge audience of your own distributors and getting a thunderous round of applause. See yourself living the lifestyle you are working and aiming for – driving that BMW or picking grapes from your own vineyard – whatever your aim is. Visualise yourself emerging from the sea on a Caribbean beach, dripping like Bo Derek or James Bond. What are you on – a six-month holiday?

Is that a warm glow or what?

Take some time to 'outcome' what your life is going to be like five years from now if you don't change your situation. What will your house be like? What will your lifestyle be like? What will your wife or husband be saying to you? How will people look at you? How will your bank manager treat you? How will your friends look at you? Does it feel good to be in the same situation as you are in just now?

Now 'outcome' the opposite. You are a successful distributor with a huge organisation and a strong six-figure income. What will your house be like? What will your lifestyle be like? What will your wife or husband be saying to you? How will people look at you? How will your bank manager be treating you? What kind of car are you driving? How will your friends look at you? Does it feel good to be in this situation? Does it feel good to have achieved your aims?

Are you going to go to work now? The aims don't just come on their own. In most businesses they wouldn't come at all, but in this business the only limit to your success is your own imagination.

Do you want massive results? Then take massive action.

Do it now!

Got the picture?

The autobiographical method

There is another method of developing the aims in your life that can be utilised by those who enjoy it. Write your own life story. It is only for your own use so it doesn't have to be of a professional standard. Start in the normal way at the beginning and include every important incident that you can remember up to the present date. It is one of the best ways of really learning about yourself. It also gives you a release for all the pent-up emotions and frustrations of your life. There is enormous therapeutic value to getting these things out in the open.

Now comes the clever bit. You have reached the present day, so how does that help you formulate your aims? The answer is to keep on going. Write the rest of your life story – the bit that has not happened yet. Write down all the things you want from life as if they have already happened. Go for the ideal. Give yourself something to live and work for. Give your life a sense of direction. make a story of it. Aim as high as you like. Remember, the only thing limiting you is your imagination.

What is life like for you – one year, five years, ten years into the future? What are you like? How have you developed? Where are you living? Imagine your home in all of its detail. What new hobbies are you following? See yourself doing them. How much have you in the bank? Visualise yourself counting it and spending it. What are you driving or flying? Strap yourself in and have the time of your life. Who are your friends? What is your wife or husband saying?

What are your children doing? Does your daughter have the pony she always wanted? You bet!

What kind of respect do you have in the community? A wealthy person like you is bound to have influence.

Have you put your future life down in writing? If so, you may have noticed that a certain fear arose in your mind in the process of your story development. I will name it for you – it is self-doubt. Ambitious, long-term aims may seem like imagining yourself winning the lottery and to be just as unlikely, but there is one major difference, you can *work* towards your aims whereas you must rely on *luck* to win the lottery. Face it, most of us have to make our own luck.

Dealing with self-doubt

Self-doubt can destroy you. I have seen it pull down the strongest of people and they all come out with a similar tale of woe – 'I just couldn't see myself making it really big,' or 'I was scared of failing, so I decided to go back to something safe, with a steady income'.

If you allow the seed thought of failure to grow in your head, then it will become a full crop of thoughts which will take over your mind and cause that very thing which you are dreading.

In the past, before I learned to deal with it, I lost opportunities – and a lot of money, because of self-doubt. Don't kid yourself. You suffer from it too!

Everyone does to some extent. Dealing with self-doubt is a matter of attacking the problem at source. The opposite of self-doubt is self-belief. You can attack the doubts by programming self-belief into your personality in the place where self-doubt would normally reside. There will then be nowhere for doubt to take root. Here are some self-programming phrases to repeat at least six times every day:

- **I am successful.**
- **I can and I will.**
- **I am the best I can possibly be.**
- **I am doing the business.**

And don't forget the one that works perhaps best of all – that old favourite given to us by Emile Coue – 'Day by day in every way, I'm getting better and better.'

No one who uses self-programming in this way can keep a poor self-image for long.

Before you leave this chapter I would like your signature. Please read over the following two sentences and sign in the appropriate place:

I have read this chapter and written down all my aims. I will stead-fastly work towards the achievement of them and thus progress towards the success that is inevitable.

SIGNED _____ DATE_____

I have read this chapter, ignored the advice and failed to write down my aims, therefore I accept that I am unlikely to succeed in life. I have let the chance slip past me.

SIGNED _____ DATE_____

IN BRIEF

This chapter has shown you:

- **how to set your aims for life**

- **the importance of persistence**

- **visualisation and outcoming**

- **how to stay focused**

- **how to revise your aims**

- **how to deal with self-doubt**

- **how to programme yourself for success**

- **how to make a commitment.**

NOTES, IDEAS AND THINGS TO DO

NOTES, IDEAS AND THINGS TO DO

–2–

CHECK IT OUT

So you now have your aims in life written down. You have photographs of your objects of desire. You want these things truly, madly and deeply. The rest of this book is about how you can achieve these aims.

If you are already involved with a company, read on. If you are not yet involved, the Direct Selling Association can provide a list of companies (see page 254). Write, requesting information and the contact name of your nearest successful distributor.

Before you start in a network marketing business you have some decisions that you must make. Ask yourself some questions.

Q 1. Are you happy that you have found the right company?

Check whether the company is a member of the Direct Selling Association (see page 254); membership ensures a high standard. Then take a good look at the company's product range. Plus points to look for concerning the company's product line:

- Universal appeal

- Only available from the company you are looking at

- Saves the customer money

- Has a health benefit

- Has snob appeal

- Has educational value

- Has a safety aspect

- Is easy to use

- Helps the environment

If the product has some of these plus points, the chances are that you are on to a winner. However, don't do a thing until you can say that each of the following statements is true:

- **You have seen the company's promotional videos**
If the company is well established there should be a few videos available. The quality and professionalism of the videos should tell you a lot about the company. If they are clearly cheap, low-budget affairs then perhaps you should suspect that the company is not what it seems. If they are very high-quality then you are probably considering a company of some standing. Bear in mind that high quality videos are a very persuasive recruiting tool. You will be able to use them yourself to build your group.

- **You have studied the company's literature**
Carefully read all the small print. If you find that the company has repeatedly written in disclaimers of its responsibilities, then make double sure that this is the right company for you before going ahead. Get your solicitor to read through everything before you sign.

- **You have tried the company's product range and are satisfied that it is of excellent quality and value for money**
If you don't like the company's product range then you will never be able to sell it convincingly. You have to love the products so much that your genuine enthusiasm communicates itself to the customers and prospects. One of the first questions that a customer will ask you is, 'Do you use the products yourself?'
    The value for money aspect is very important. You may find it difficult to sell products that are overpriced.

● **The products have a 'repeat sale' aspect**
This is our built-in 'Pension Plan'. With the best plans, customers will make their repeat sales direct from the company, with the company sending the repeat commission direct to you.

● **You have attended a business opportunity meeting (BOM) or two.** (*These are also called business seminars or briefings*).
Don't be put off on this point. If your company does not have BOMs then you may find it more difficult to recruit new distributors. BOMs can do most of the hard work of recruiting for you. All you have to do is invite people along. Take a good look at the quality of people invited and taking part. Are they your sort? Are they winners or losers? Beware of meetings filled with people straight off the streets, lured in by the offer of free coffee and biscuits.

● **You have had a personal consultation with a senior distributor of the company**
If the senior distributor above your sponsor can't be bothered to meet you, you will have to consider the quality and quantity of back-up that you will receive. If they are not interested now, will they be interested after you have signed up and ordered stock?

● **You have checked out the company's financial stability and track record**
New companies clearly have enormous growth potential, but there is high failure rate over the first few years. A more established company will have already hit the market to a certain extent, but if they have a good track record they are more likely to be around to pay your cheques.

Look at the borrowings of a company before you get involved. Are they going to be crippled by interest payments? Are they borrowing in order to pay their distributors? If you can find a company that has never borrowed in order to expand, you will have found a rare breed among network marketing companies.

● **You are happy with the company's marketing plan and remuneration package**
Network marketing companies can offer you remuneration with a long-term build potential that goes far beyond what could be achieved in normal business. Ensure that the company has not placed an upper limit on your earnings. Avoid companies that do not conform to the general principles outlined in the marketing plan chapter (Chapter 3). You should be able to tell a self-seeking and greedy company by the enormous amount of work that you will have to do to achieve a good income.

● **You are satisfied that the business has excellent long-term potential**
Check that the market is not near saturation with the company's main product range. If there are already a large number of distributors in your area then you will clearly have to look further afield for your group expansion.

● **The company is investing substantially in research and development**
Products that do not improve will lose their appeal as competition takes over with better products. Find out how long the products have been on the market. Have any improvements been made? Are any overdue? Are the products 'state of the art' or are they already a few years behind the latest on the market?

● **The company is committed to bringing new products on line**
This is essential for your long-term development; otherwise, when all your target market has been hit with existing products, you will have insurmountable problems. You will have nothing new to offer.

● **The company is licensed to operate internationally.** (Ideally).
For unlimited potential you need an unlimited market.

All true? If you have found a company that stands up to this scrutiny then you have found a very successful and stable company. Such companies exist. Why choose less?

The information that you have acquired by doing your check will be of enormous use when the time comes for you to help others to make the decision to join you. Absolutely scrupulous honesty must be your standard at all times, both with yourself and others. Some propositions can look so inviting that the temptation is to overlook the weaknesses in the company. Don't fall into that trap.

Once your company has been thoroughly checked out, you will have to decide how much product you will require. Your sponsor should help you to make up a product package to suit your individual needs, but there are some things you should consider before taking your product decision.

Q 2. How fast do you want to achieve success?

Are you happy to potter along taking things nice and easy, working at your own relaxed pace – or do you want success yesterday? Network marketing is a low risk business compared to most. The one thing you do need to risk is your time. The more time you are willing to give this business, the more profit it is willing to give you, but the relationship is not always directly proportional. For a very little time devoted to the sales aspect, good profits are available. By working only one or two nights a week, it is possible to build up a small team under your supervision which could be – in the words of Arthur Daley – 'A nice little earner!'

It is when you want to get into the serious money that you have to devote serious time to the business. In order to decide how much money you will make, you must first decide how much time you will devote to the business.

Q 3. Where do you see yourself in the business?

Do you want to achieve a position such as direct distributor? In many companies you deal only with your sponsor until you achieve a certain rebate level, at which time you become a 'direct', and are qualified to deal direct with the company.

Take a good look at the marketing plan and decide what rebate level you would like to work at. With the best plans, when you reach a certain rebate level you will not drop back down again. For instance, if you order £3,000 worth of product you may qualify for a 20 per cent or 25 per cent rebate level, but if you only order £1,000 worth then you may only qualify for a 10 per cent rebate.

The test of a really good marketing plan is this: What happens if you don't order the same or more the next month? Does the rebate level drop back down so that you have to requalify all over again, or does it stay where it is? If it stays, then there is a fair chance that you have found a good plan. For greater knowledge of what constitutes a good plan, read Chapter 3.

Q 4. How much product do you need to keep you busy for the time that you are willing to give?

The more time that you can devote to the business the more product you will need, but if you are only willing to devote a few hours a week to the business you can keep a very low stock level.

The other important factor is how much product can you afford? It is good sense to order as much as you can afford on your initial order in order to achieve a higher rebate level from the start, but never buy more than you know you will be able to shift personally. Some companies have massive 'buy back' problems because they allow people to buy too much too soon. Only recently have they started to get to grips with the problem and realise that they must move the stock on to the consumer in order to be successful long-term.

That said, in some marketing plans your profit can double according to the rebate level that you are on. So get together with your sponsor, or, if he is fairly new into the business, get together with someone 'upline' from him and decide where you want to start off.

Remember, the final decision must be yours. You don't have to accept any recommendation, but you would be well advised to listen. Network marketing is a very ethical business and your sponsor is unlikely to suggest an unsuitable package for you. After all, it is in his own interest that you become successful as he will be getting a percentage of your order value.

However, there are conmen in every profession and network marketing has its share. Usually the cheats don't last long, and that is where the trouble comes in. If you have been sponsored by someone who is on his way out, then that person may try to offload unsaleable stock in your direction. If you have investigated the opportunity properly then it should be obvious if your sponsor is suggesting stock that the rest of the distributors don't seem to be using. If you suspect something is wrong, then ask for a second or third opinion.

Q 5. How many trainings are you willing to attend in your first four months?

Your sponsor will slot you into the company training seminars and lectures. I would advise you to go to as many as you can possibly attend for the first month or two, in order to give you a sound understanding of the company. You should also watch the company videos and listen to motivational audio tapes. It will soon become clear to your sponsor if you are going to be successful. If you can't be bothered to turn up to the trainings then you are going to become one of the 80 per cent dropouts. All too often new distributors attend one or two training sessions and then think that they know it all.

If you want to be really successful, you should also attend the company's regional and national trainings if they have them. You will get the 'big picture' there, and be able to listen to some of the most successful trainers in the world. If you are tempted to miss one then ask yourself this, 'Would I go if there were £1,000 waiting for me there?' If the answer is 'yes' then go, because in the long run the information that you gain will be worth a lot more than £1,000.

- **It is true to say that not all those who attend the trainings are successful, but all those who are successful attend the trainings.**
Coincidence? I don't think so.

If you have answered the five questions above and are happy with what you have learned, then go ahead and order your product.

Now is the time to do your homework. When you have finished with this book, get hold of as many books on self-improvement, multi-level marketing and network marketing as you can. There is a reading list at the end of this book. You must become an expert as soon as possible. If you really want to be successful in this business, you will need to learn enough about it to be able to teach others. That won't happen in the week or so between ordering your product and waiting for it to arrive, so the sooner you start the better.

You will have to accept that there will be a learning period of many months, or even years. Network marketing is a reflection of life; if you stop learning you start dying. In this business you had better be teachable! If you are not, don't bother starting. The successful network marketing organisations are generally those which have been around for a number of years. They have learned the hard way and are feeding huge sums into training so that their distributors can avoid all the mistakes that have been made in the past.

Those who want their group to be really successful will eventually start their own training sessions. That means you. Read how to do it in Chapter 20.

IN BRIEF

This chapter has shown you:

- **which points to check**

- **how to decide on the initial order**

- **the training commitment**

- **how to cope with the learning period.**

NOTES, IDEAS AND THINGS TO DO

– 3 –

THE MARKETING PLAN AND DISTRIBUTOR CONTRACT

If you haven't read the introduction yet, go back and read it now.

This is a very simple business to understand. So simple that it is often dismissed as ridiculous or outrageous. It is too good to be true, but it *is* true. More people have made more money in network marketing over the last ten years than in any other business in the world.

There are a number of ways to approach the business. If you are the manufacturer or the sole importer of a unique range of products you could start your own network marketing organisation to distribute them.

If you are already involved in a non-compatible business, or if you work for someone else and you are trapped in a lifestyle of only limited potential, you could key into an existing network marketing business as an additional income source. In this way, you become affiliated to an already successful company, but retain the benefits of self-employment.

No prior knowledge necessary

I am not going to assume any prior knowledge on your part, so I will use a mythical product to explain how network marketing works. Say, for example, that someone has invented an ever-lasting lightbulb and it is being marketed the network way. The marketing plan shown in this chapter will show how you could benefit by building a team to market the bulbs. You should also come to understand how, with hundreds or perhaps thousands of other distributors doing the same as you, the bulb company can rapidly achieve a high turnover with incredibly low overheads. That is why network marketing companies are so supportive to their distributors and the reason that they can pass on so much profit from the product to their distributors. You become their only cost of expansion. It pays the company to help you build your business because it means more business for them. You work together as part of a team for the mutual benefit.

Because of the mass of facts and figures that need to be absorbed, this is probably the most difficult chapter to read and follow. If you want to skip the rest of the chapter and come back to it later than I will forgive you, but *do* come back to it. Otherwise there will be a gap in your knowledge that you may never fill.

Preliminary study

Before you sign on with a network marketing company you should get a copy of their marketing plan. Study it carefully and, if necessary, get your solicitor or accountant to look it over. There are con artists out there just waiting for the right person to give them easy money. Having said that, the vast majority of successful network marketing companies are highly ethical organisations with marketing plans that stand up to the closest scrutiny.

Don't confuse the marketing plan which explains your chosen network marketing company's methods of business with your own business plan. Your business plan is covered in Chapter 10.

The marketing plan will show you that the business is structured on a number of levels, hence the term multi-level marketing which is sometimes used for the business. Each level is reached when your turnover achieves a monthly wholesale target figure. Thus, to achieve a particular level you and your group have to purchase the target value of product from the company. In some companies you may be able to buy into 'a position' by personally purchasing your monthly target figure. If you can afford to do that it could get you a good discount/bonus level, but beware of buying more product than you can be sure of selling or passing on to those you recruit into your group. Never buy into a position when you are a beginner. You won't have the experience needed to take advantage of the position, and you won't have the wholesale buying/retail selling power of a downline behind you to earn you a regular income.

A warning

Beware also of certain unethical companies who encourage their distributors to persuade new recruits to take huge amounts of stock in the usually mistaken understanding that they will recoup it all very quickly. Remember that network marketing is a long-term business, and not a 'get rich quick' scheme. Anyone who tells you otherwise is lying to you. This is also a warning to readers to resist the temptation of trying to off-load large amounts of stock on new dealers. You may make a quick wholesale profit this way, but it will almost certainly be clawed back when your dealers find that they cannot sell the goods as easily as they thought, and they decide to get 90 per cent of their money back by returning the goods to the company[1]. It is far better to start them off humbly, teach them how to sell and thus create a successful member of your organisation. They will soon enough order large amounts of stock when they know they can sell it.

The really ethical companies put a restriction on the amount of goods that you can purchase for resale in the first month, and at the time of writing, according to restrictions imposed on network marketing companies under the Fair Trading Act, there is a limit on the value of goods you can purchase in the first seven days after signing up. More details of the law later in this chapter. Certain companies insist that you have to prove to them that you can sell, or have sold your product or a portion of your product to retail customers before you get your rebates. This is to ensure that the business builds properly through retail sales rather than purely through networking. The rocks upon which all businesses are built are retail sales. Any business that fails to get properly through to the customer base won't last long.

[1] New regulations currently under consideration are likely to either restrict the automatic right to refund to 30 days after purchase, or to remove the refund right entirely, leaving this matter to the discretion of the companies. Read your distributor contract carefully. The terms on your contract when you signed up will continue to apply to you unless you agree to a new contract.

Typical network marketing sales targets

Senior co-ordinating distributor target £24,000/month

Co-ordinating Distributor target £12,000/month

Bonus distributor target £6,000/month

Direct distributor target £3,000/month

Ordinary distributor no minimum target

The names and target levels may vary from company to company, but the positions are roughly comparable.

At the top of the ladder, the senior co-ordinating distributor will have developed a huge network with a number of co-ordinating distributors in his or her group. Each of these co-ordinating distributors will have a number of bonus distributors in his or her group. Each bonus distributor will have a number of direct distributors in his or her group. Each direct distributor will have a number of ordinary distributors in his or her group. At the bottom of the ladder, each ordinary distributor can have a number of other ordinary distributors in his or her group.

There will be hundreds, perhaps thousands, of ordinary distributors to every senior co-ordinating distributor, so if the senior co-ordinating distributor is getting 2 or 3 per cent of the turnover of his or her whole group, you can see how an embarrassingly large income can develop. This long-term potential is what motivates the whole group. They won't all achieve it. Most of them won't bother even to find out how to achieve it. Of those who do find out how to achieve it, most still won't do what it takes. This book will show you how to do it. It is really up to you what you do with the information.

How the money grows

The basic principle is that everyone buys the product at the same price, but the further up the ladder you get, the bigger the rebate level you achieve. Let's say the everlasting lightbulbs (ELBs) are £5 wholesale and £6.50 retail. That is approximately 23 per cent profit margin at the lowest level.

The company will provide a rebate table as part of their marketing plan. If facts and figures don't interest you, skip this bit. But if you really want to get down to the nitty-gritty then study it carefully.

The version shown here is necessarily a simplified form as various marketing plans each have their own complicating factors.

Wholesale volume of ELBs purchased/month

£		Rebate	Bonus	Total Profit
100	It should be noted that some companies provide	0%	0%	23%
500	discounts rather than rebates. In these cases,	5%	0%	28%
1,000	*discount differential* is equal to wholesale profit.	7%	0%	30%
2,000	Qualifies as direct distributor	10%	0%	33%
3,000	Qualifies as bonus distributor	10%	3%	36%
6,000	Qualifies as co-ordinating distributor	10%	5%	38%
24,000	Qualifies as senior co-ordinating distributor	10%	7%	40%
56,000	Qualifies as gold co-ordinating distributor	10%	8%	41%

There will probably also be group requirements for various levels such as having to have three co-ordinating distributors (CDs) in your group and six continuous months' volume requirements to qualify as a senior co-ordinating distributor (SCD).

In the above illustration, the company has rewarded a qualifying SCD with a percentage of the wholesale volume that goes through the qualifying CDs.

Some companies have introduced even more senior positions such as national marketing directors, who enjoy such benefits as profit sharing, expense accounts, health insurance and free education packages.

Monthly volume

When you look at the volume requirement of £56,000 to qualify as a GCD, it may seem impossible to achieve, but don't forget this is the requirement for you and your whole team. Let's look at how high volume can be achieved.

The object is to develop a group by getting one person a month, and teaching that person to do the same and so on. But with one highly committed person every two months or every six months, the system still works, and is self-replicating. For simplicity we will assume that each new distributor orders £100 of ELBs to get started and, having sold that stock, thus proving that the business is viable, orders £1,000 worth and reorders the same volume each month. We will ignore the initial £100 orders.

The following table is idealised. It is simply a representation of how exponential growth can have astonishing results.

Month	Distributors	Wholesale Value
1	self	1,000
2	2	2,000
3	4	4,000
4	8	8,000
5	16	16,000
6	32	32,000
7	64	64,000
8	132	132,000

Commonly, 3 per cent of the wholesale value will be paid to each level of distributor. The remaining parts of the bonus will be paid on personal orders for product, and as bonuses for qualification to different levels, but we will ignore these for the sake of simplicity.

Still working from the above plan, looking at month 6, if a new SCD has qualified in this month, as a total volume of £32,000 would permit, he or she will be rewarded as follows:

3% of £32,000 = £960 (total group volume)
2% of £6,000 = £120 (the 5% bonus level)
2% of £24,000 = £480 (the 7% bonus level)
          Total = £1,560 income for this month – by
                  most standards a good living wage.

This total does not include the profit from personal sales made, or the additional bonuses from personally introduced and newly qualified bonus distributors or ordinary distributors. It also does not include the wholesale profit made when wholesaling stock to ordinary distributors. Remember, a GCD makes 41 per cent profit on his or her stock, but a new distributor makes only 23 per cent profit, so when a GCD supplies stock to a distributor, he makes 18 per cent clear profit. If a new distributor buys £1,000 of stock from a GCD to get started, the SCD makes £180 in that one transaction.

Such wholesale profit is the power behind network marketing.

Of course, only exceptional individuals can achieve these levels in a short space of time, but even if you only achieve a small percentage of this – say a tenth, work out for yourself the size of profit you will make in a year.

Now work it out for five years into the future.

Impressed? Do you want that sort of income?

Let's look now at a five-year plan to make £1 million per year based only on the 3 per cent minimum, and assuming each distributor manages only £1,000 sales per month and recruits five new distributors per year. Bear in mind that this is idealised. No real structure will look like this.

Year	New distributors	£ Volume/month	3%
1	5	5,000	150
2	25	25,000	750
3	125	125,000	3,750
4	625	625,000	18,750
5	3,125	3,125,000	93,750

At the end of five years the 3 per cent alone gives £93,750 per month which is £1,125,000 per year. Bonuses and other benefits would bring your income up to £1.3 million per year!

That profit level is available to *anyone* who will do what it takes. All you have to do is sell your product, get five people a year into the business and teach them to do the same. That is all there is to it. The marketing plan may be complicated, but the business is simple – so simple that if you follow the simple rules and work very hard and, above all, persist, success is inevitable.

Buying into a position

Some companies permit new distributors to 'buy into a position'. What this means is that by purchasing a certain amount of stock, you can instantly obtain the position and discount level for which your investment qualifies you. For example, in order to qualify for the position of, say, co-ordinating distributor, it may be necessary to order £24,000 worth of stock in one calendar month and have three active legs. The normal way, and by far the best way to achieve this, is to have built up the business from scratch so that the total monthly purchase volume through your line (from your personal purchases to supply your downline and from qualified direct purchases from your downline) equals or surpasses the required £24,000.

On the other hand, the 'buying in' way to achieve the same position is simply to hand over the £24,000 to the company. There are a number of ways to get round the problem of having 'active legs', the most common of which is to sign members of your family below you in your line, and later, when you have made contacts and started recruiting, you can transfer or sell the enrolment number and part of your stock to your new recruit.

The snag with taking the second route to network marketing success is that unless you have been with a previous company, you will have no experience in network marketing. Think of it – most of those who have worked their way up to the level that you have just bought into will be turning over that amount of stock every month. Their income comes from that. They have a team. You don't. You have to go out and find your team. What are you going to do for income in the meantime? I know a man who lost £30,000 trying to buy his way to success in this way. He was an excellent salesman, but he knew nothing about network marketing. He made all his mistakes the expensive way. Now he is lost to network marketing for ever.

If he had started more modestly with a small investment in stock, and gradually learned the business while continuing his normal job, I am certain that I would now be using his example as a success story.

There is another side to buying into a position. The instant prestige and credibility that the purchased position gives you can seriously help your recruiting. New prospects will look to you as a successful example of what they can achieve with a little work. Some people have made it really big after buying into a position. It is a fast way to start for real high-flyers. It is risky, but if you don't mind the risk, if you can afford it and if you like jumping in at the deep end . . . go for it.

BUT, don't give up your daytime job until you are certain that your income from network marketing is sufficient to keep you. Think ahead. What would happen if your top person decided to change companies? You need a sufficiently developed team both in depth and width so that your business will not be destroyed by one or more people dropping out. Remember, too, that when a drop-out occurs, and one of your downline sells his or her stock back to the company, your commission/rebate will be clawed back. This is another good reason to help them become successful.

The new distributor contract

According to the wide ranging Fair Trading Act, every advert, prospectus, circular or notice, which indicates the financial benefits available through a network marketing company, must contain an easily visible statutory warning containing the following information:

1. Make sure that you understand what is being offered to you.

2. Do not be misled by claims that high earnings are easily achieved.

3. It is advisable to take independent legal advice before signing a contract.

The advertisement must also show the date on which the company started operating in the UK, the name and address of the promoter(s), a description of the goods or services covered by the scheme and the nature of the business opportunity.

[2]If earnings claims are made as to earnings attainable during any period, the claim must be accompanied by the statement, 'The figures shown do not represent any automatic earnings. Actual earnings will depend on time and effort spent on the business and the total number of participants in the scheme'.

If training is offered it must be pointed out that it is voluntary and any charge must be made clear in advance.

---

[2] Under the new regulations currently being considered, the wording of the warnings is being changed, but will have the same aim of protecting overenthusiastic beginners.

If the company makes no claim as to financial benefits on the contract, then the company can get away without the statutory warning, but you will find that most companies, being ethical by nature, will have the warning included on their contracts. Most contracts will also include details of your rights.

Rights

In addition to the above, every participant in a network marketing operation has certain statutory rights (currently under review).

1. You have the right to pull out of the operation without penalty.

2. If you withdraw within fourteen days of joining, you are entitled by law to a refund in full of all money you have paid to join, and of the full value of any unsold and undamaged goods which you return.

3. After the first fourteen days, if you pull out and return the goods, the network marketing company can deduct from the refund any amount paid to you or due to you for goods sold or not returned. They can also deduct for deterioration of the goods if this was your fault.

4. After this period you can still leave the scheme at any time, but in addition to the deductions above, the company can deduct a handling fee.

Illegal payments

You earn your money in network marketing by sales profits, and by bonuses and rebates for orders placed by yourself and your team.

Any money which you pay out is either for registration with the company, for stock which you have ordered, or for training.

It is illegal for anyone to ask you for payment *without giving you anything in return*, simply because they tell you that you stand to gain from recruitment. If anyone asks you for such a payment they are committing a criminal offence.

Bear in mind that there are some companies that do not require you to buy stock, but rather they enrol you on a scheme where they automatically stack those who enrol after you, below you in a straight downline. With large numbers of people enrolled, they generate interest, and thus commissions and profits, for you with sometimes astonishingly large sums of money being paid. There are many variations on this method. A very few are genuine. Some are dubious, bordering on the illegal, others are little more than disguised endowment insurance schemes without the advantages of life cover, with the very large payments taking many years before they 'mature'. *Make sure that you know what you are getting into.* Don't be deceived by glossy brochures.

During your first seven days after signing up, since the Fair Trading Act prevents the company from selling more than a limited value of goods to you (both the value and the timescale are currently under review), it is illegal for anyone (in connection with the company) to receive more than that sum from you for goods. The offence is theirs, of course, not yours.

If you make a deposit or security on goods ordered, it must be refundable if you return the goods in original condition.

If you find yourself getting involved with a firm that is flouting the above requirements then you should carefully consider if you want to be a part of what they are doing.

Having said all that, it would be fair of me to point out that all established companies have sorted out the above long ago and that they are extremely unlikely to breach the law in any way. On the contrary, they go out of their way to be extremely fair to their distributors, since after all, only by giving you every chance to succeed can they succeed themselves.

IN BRIEF

This chapter has shown you:

- **how to understand the marketing plan**
- **how to understand the distributor contract**
- **how to buy into a position**
- **your rights under the law**
- **the five-year plan to make a million per year**
- **illegal payments: don't get caught out.**

NOTES, IDEAS AND THINGS TO DO

-4-

YOUR PROSPECT LIST

Those organisations which offer no training tend to be much less successful than those which do. Successful training breeds successful distributors. Successful distributors make a successful company. If you are looking at companies trying to decide which one to choose, then do yourself a large favour if possible and choose one with training facilities within an hour's travel of your home. That said, however, I know of distributors who travel hundreds of miles each week to training.

Are they successful? Of course they are. That sort of commitment is what sorts out the winners from the losers. Someone willing to travel hundreds of miles to training is going to listen very carefully to what is said there and put all the advice into action.

We will be going into the details of training later, but right now I know you are dying to find out how this business operates.

Taking action

To put together your initial prospect list, write down the name, address and telephone number of everyone that you know. This prospect list should contain at least 100 names and preferably 200. You don't think you know that many?

Think about it. How many people do you know in the city or town where you live? Put all their names down. It doesn't matter if the person is a little old lady or a successful business-person. A little old lady may have a son who is a successful businessman and he may provide you with a dozen valuable contacts. Write the names down if you know the person, even if you have only spoken to them once. Even, in fact if you have only nodded to them.

The company may provide you with a memory jogger which will help you recall names such as:

> Friends, relatives, workmates past and present, schoolfriends, penfriends, business associates, people who bill you such as the baker, dentist, milkman, grocer. Teachers at your children's school, people you meet only socially, hotel and bar keepers, people at your golf club, chess club, darts club, bridge club.

I could fill pages with prompters alone, but you can use your imagination and find them for yourself. If you really find yourself stuck, pick up your local phone directory and go through it, starting at A. What does it start at – Adam? Do you know anyone called Adam? Put him down. Are his parents alive? Put them down. What does he do? Who else do you know who does that? Put them down. Do they have any brothers or sisters? Put them down. Where do they live, Birmingham? Who else do you know who lives in Birmingham? Put them down.

I can guarantee that unless you have lived your whole life on a desert island you will find at least 100 names before you even get to C.

Do you have your list together? Minimum 100 and preferably 200 names? Good. Now, please, please take this piece of advice: whatever you do, don't go out and start contacting them until you have had some training. You will tell them all the wrong things and lose potentially valuable customers and distributors before you even get started. Believe me, I speak from experience. It is easy to get excited by the prospect of making massive sales to all these people on your list whom you are sure will buy from you, but you can't sell your product over the telephone, you can't answer their questions if you don't know the answers and you can't deal with their objections if you haven't learned the techniques.

Network marketing is a direct sales business. When the time comes for you to sell, let the prospect see, feel and, if possible, use the product. If it is really good, the prospect will want it. Don't try to sell before you have read the sales chapter in this book (Chapter 8).

In this consumer society, scepticism abounds, but:

- tell them about it and they will hear you;

- show them and they will see you;

- let them use it and they will believe you.

First things first. Before you contact anyone you have to grade the list to decide whom to approach first about the business and whom to approach about the product.

Prospect grading

We are going to grade your prospects according to seven points: A, B, C1, C2, D, E and F. At the end of the grading you will add up the points of each prospect, and decide whom to approach about the business and whom to approach about the product.

A is for **Attitude**. Does the prospect have a good attitude or is the prospect a negative person? If the prospect is the sort to fly into a bad mood when things don't go the right way, you don't want such a person in your business. On the other hand, if the prospect is positive thinking and good humoured, give that person a tick.

B is for **Businessperson** or **Businesslike**. Is the prospect already self-employed or someone who could see the potential of network marketing? Tick.

C1 is for **Credibility**. Does the prospect have credibility with other people? Tick.

C2 is for **Contacts**. Does the prospect have a good circle of contacts? Tick.

D for **Desire**. Does the prospect have the desire for better circumstances? Tick.

E for **Educatable** or teachable. If the prospect is a know-it-all then it is a waste of time recruiting that person into the business because that person will fail. Give a tick if the prospect is educatable.

F for **Finance**. It is preferable that your prospect has a good financial situation, but this is possibly the least important qualification. If the prospect wants success badly enough to do what it takes, then little else matters.

Now look at the list and pick out your top twenty – those with the most ticks. The others will be approached with the products and we will go into details of that in the sales chapter, but these top twenty are the people whom you are going to approach with the business first. If there are company business introduction seminars or briefings in your area, invite them to attend rather than trying to do all the work yourself, but don't invite them all at once. If there are no such seminars in your area, or rather, in the area where the prospect lives, then you may find it more convenient to let your prospect watch a company video as a first introduction to the business.

To say or not to say?

What you say to your top prospects is very important. Try to allow people to discover the business for themselves. Remember, you are only making an appointment. Don't try to sell the business over the telephone. If you do try that then you will certainly fail. Many of the concepts of network marketing are visual and almost impossible to communicate over the telephone.

Here are a few sample scripts for use when telephoning to set up a meeting with your prospect.

'Hi Dave, it's John. Listen, I'll tell you why I'm phoning, I've just started this little business of my own and I need a bit of help in understanding the concepts. I know you are running your own business and I thought you would be the right person to give me some advice. Could you meet me on Wednesday night at the Big Bear Hotel and we could discuss things?'

When Dave comes along you will introduce him to your sponsor who will show Dave the basic concepts, ostensibly so that he can check it out for you. Being smart, and everything else being what it should be, Dave will begin to be impressed by the potential of the business and your sponsor can say to Dave:

'Hey Dave, I know you came along to check this out for John, but you seem pretty interested yourself. Maybe you'd like to look at it as a possible sideline along with what you are already doing?'

That is the 'help' tack. If Dave is a friend of yours then he is not going to refuse to help you. This business has such enormous potential that you have to introduce people to the concepts gently. Don't go phoning your friends and start trying to tell them all about the business and, don't worry, your sponsor is unlikely to try to steal your prospects. When the time comes for your prospect to sign up, your name will be on the form as the 'sponsor', so you will have begun the process of building a group.

Here is a script NOT to use when you contact your friend!

'Hi Dave, it's John. Listen, there is something I just have to tell you about. It's fantastic. I've found this business where you can earn over a million pounds a year. It's selling these fantastic everlasting lightbulbs that hardly use any electricity. I'll be driving a Rolls in a month. I want you to come into the business with me because I know that you could do with a million a year as much as I could.'

On the face of it this script seems not too bad. Have another look at it and try to figure out what is wrong with it.

You've got it. It's far too enthusiastic. You can't take someone who is earning average money and offer them an opportunity to earn a million a year. They will think you have flipped. Gently does it.

Here is another possible script that DOES work

> 'Hi Dave, it's John. Listen, do you have time to earn a bit of extra cash along with your existing job? You do. Good. How about meeting me for coffee tonight and we can have a chat.'

If Dave asks what it is all about, tell him that you have just started yourself and don't know much about it yet, but you have invited an expert along who will explain the business.

When Dave turns up he will find that your sponsor is there too. Let your sponsor do most of the talking. Remember – the stranger is the expert. Your friend will listen to your sponsor much more seriously than he will listen to you if you are discussing a new business concept, unless you have a business reputation of very high standing.

Now I am going to tell you the approach that works best of all with friends.

> 'Hi Dave, it's John. Let's meet for a drink at the club tonight. Great. See you at seven.'

When Dave comes along, ask him how he is doing. Listen carefully to what he says, because you may get a lot of hints that you will be able to use in introducing the business concepts to him. After he tells you how he is doing, he will usually ask you the same thing. There is your opening:

> 'I'm doing great. In fact I've just got started in a new business . . .'

Let Dave ask you about it. If he is smart he will gradually uncover something that interests him and, best of all, he will think that finding out about it is his own idea.

Now for an example of a cold call by telephone

'Good afternoon Mr Smith. My name is John Watson. I am involved with a firm that is developing a number of secondary profit centres for business people in this area. Could you meet me for a coffee tonight in the Big Bear Hotel so that we can discuss a possible project for yourself?'

Inevitably he will ask what it is all about. So you say:

'I'd rather not discuss the details over the telephone. The business concepts are 90 per cent visual.'

Just make the appointment. If the prospect insists on getting details over the telephone then the chances are that he or she would be no use at this business anyway. We need people with open minds. At the meeting, ensure that visual aids do predominate the meeting. Honesty is essential to win confidence.

So, we have established that one of the keys to success is:

'Don't allow yourself to be tricked into releasing details about your business over the telephone.'

On the other hand, many successful distributors have built their business using the telephone as their main tool. You can invite many people by telephone in the same time that it takes you to invite one person whom you have to visit to invite. With prospects that you don't know very well, this is primarily a numbers game. Here is a formula which will act as a rough guide of just how much work you have to do:

- talk to three and one will listen;
- three listen and one will attend a business briefing;
- three attend and one will join the business;
- three join the business and one will be successful;
- three are successful and one will be very successful.

Will that be you?

At a training session where I was invited to take a slot on self-motivation, I heard a very successful network marketing distributor and trainer use a phrase that really caught the imagination: 'You are the one who used to boast that you'd be the one who would do the most.'

Could you read that line, and then sit back and relax and say, 'I'll do it later'?

Do it now!

Finding new prospects

You should always be adding new names to your prospect list. As soon as you stop doing that, unless you have built a very successful business, a process of decay will start that could end in your failure.

It is so easy to find new names that you need never run out. Starting small, you can put an advert in the window of local shops and or in local newspapers. When you have more money available you can advertise in national newspapers in every country in which your company operates.

As previously mentioned, although not all companies approve of their use, you can purchase mailing lists which you will find advertised in magazines devoted to business opportunities, and mail order. Mailing lists of people who have responded to network marketing or business opportunity adverts in the past can bring a very high response rate used in conjunction with the type of letters discussed in Chapter 9.

Luck can play in your success, but mostly you have to make your own luck. Everyone is a prospect and the successful network builder never stops looking. Remember the one-in-three rule. When you work out all the one-in-threes that apply, it means that of all the people whom you approach with the business, only one in 250 is going to become very successful. You need at least three and preferably five very successful distributors in your 'frontline' (meaning that you have personally recruited them). This means that before you can have a really successful network marketing business you will need to personally approach between 750 and 1,250 viable prospects with the business opportunity.

If you are already involved in network marketing and haven't yet made a success of it, then you know now what you have to do! It may seem like an impossible task, but many other people have achieved it and so can you. It is simply a numbers game. Can you manage to approach just one person a day? Then in three years you will have introduced the network marketing concept to over a thousand people, and will have built yourself a substantial and highly profitable business.

Never stop looking

Are you in the habit of taking an empty table when you go into a restaurant on your own? It is so easy to make new friends. All you have to do is sit down and say, 'Mind if I join you? I hate eating alone.'

Similarly, when you board a train or plane, never sit alone. Some of the best contacts you can make are fellow travellers. You don't have to book an appointment with them. They have time to spare. Don't let the opportunity pass without telling them about the business, but first you have to create an empathy with them. People love good listeners. Ask them what they do. Find out if there is any area of their business that they are unhappy with. After they have told you and you have proved how fascinating a personality you have by saying very little and listening intently to them, you may find that they ask you what you do. You win or lose them with your answer, but don't go straight into your business presentation. You have to intrigue people and let them pull the answers from you in order to satisfy their curiosity.

Here's an example of how to handle it, Mary is our distributor, Ken is the prospect:

Ken: 'What do you do?'
Mary: 'I'm in the wealth creation business.'

Ken: 'Sounds intriguing.'
Mary: 'It is.'

Ken: 'How do you create wealth?'
Mary: 'We take a product line and market it through a unique system that has made our company one of the most successful in the world.'

Ken: 'What system is that?'

Mary then takes out her folder and outlines the business concepts, shaping the business to appeal particularly to Ken. She already knows what interests Ken. She already knows what Ken dislikes about his present line of work.

- If he would like more free time then she tells him about the twenty weeks' holiday per year that top distributors can achieve.

- If money is his motivator then she particularly concentrates on the long-term financial benefits.

- If job satisfaction is what Ken would like then Mary tells him about the very real satisfaction of helping others achieve success.

- If he doesn't get enough responsibility in his present job then Mary tells him about the responsibility of running a team.

- If Ken appears to lack self-confidence then Mary tells him about the personal growth that takes place in people who join our business.

- If Ken just hates his job then Mary concentrates on the fun and social side of network marketing. I know of as many people who were attracted to the business because of the fun they had at our seminars and trainings, as were attracted because of the money.

Extra 'ordinary'

When considering whom to approach with the business, do not aim only for those prospects whom you consider to be of high quality. After all, most 'ordinary' people have hidden or unexploited talents. It is your job to help those people to reach inside and pull out those suppressed abilities. Most of the top distributors in network marketing are – or rather were – 'ordinary' people whose latent ability and sheer hard work took them to the top. Ordinary people are the life-blood of network marketing. Within each ordinary person is an extraordinary person just waiting to be discovered. Part of your task will be to help people believe in themselves and in their own abilities. Show them how to dress. Teach them what to say. Let them discover the wonderful feeling of helping others achieve success. Help them achieve the good things in life and you will see them change before your eyes, growing in confidence and networking ability each day. All this depends on one thing. Teachability. If the prospect is teachable, anything is possible.

Build deep

Network marketing is essentially a copy-cat business. You copy your most successful 'upline' distributor. Your new distributors copy you and their new distributors copy them – or, and this is an important 'or', they copy you. Thus, even though the sponsor who introduces a new distributor may not succeed – usually through failure to keep to the commitments he or she has made – those the distributor has introduced can go on to succeed by copying you, instead of copying the failure. It is therefore evident that your responsibility does not stop with your 'frontline' distributors.

If you really want to succeed – if you are going for that six-figure a year income, you have to build a very deep network by helping your distributors to sort out their prospect list and recruit new distributors, and then you have to do the same with *their* prospects and so on.

It doesn't pay to abandon your new distributors to their own efforts after a short training session or two. They will fade away through lack of knowledge. Only through regular attendance at organised trainings and on-the-job training will they get the knowledge necessary. That knowledge will bring with it the belief they need and help develop the incentive that they *must* have. Only then, when they are as motivated and knowledgeable as you are, will they be ready to go it alone and even then remember that they are still part of your team. In fact, I'd go even further – they are now part of your family, so treat them as such. How far would you travel to help a member of your family in need? Don't hesitate, then, to travel to the other end of the country to help one of your distributors.

It is a fixed principle in network marketing that you can only ever succeed in building a group by helping others to achieve success.

Build wide

Personally sponsored prospects build the shoulder width that your group needs for strength. The wider your group is, the less dependent you will be on each individual. You won't then be broken hearted if one of them decides to head for what appears to be greener grass.

Contrary to popular belief, the grass is always greener on this side. There are so many companies with so many varied opportunities that if you go chasing all of them, one after another, then you will dissipate your efforts and end up achieving little or nothing. This is why many successful distributors will say that you should concentrate your efforts on one company alone.

Eggs and baskets

On the other hand there is a school of thought which says that your business is not just one company, but network marketing in general. If you are involved with a number of network marketing companies then you can offer your prospects a choice. If they don't go for one then they may go for another. They may prefer selling books or loans, instead of golf clubs or water filters. Rather than put all their eggs in one basket they may even prefer to join a number of companies themselves and duplicate what you are doing.

If you concentrate all your efforts on one company going for gold all the way then you have a very good chance of success, but you will lose a lot of prospects because they don't like the particular opportunity you are offering. You pays your money and takes your choice!

IN BRIEF

This chapter has shown you:

- **how to sort out your prospect list**
- **how to grade your prospects**
- **what to say to your prospects**
- **what not to say to them**
- **cold-calling by telephone**
- **that you should never stop looking**
- **how to find extra 'ordinary' people**
- **how to build a deep and wide network**
- **how to decide on concentration or diversification.**

NOTES, IDEAS AND THINGS TO DO

NOTES, IDEAS AND THINGS TO DO

– 5 –

TAILORING THE

BUSINESS

One of the great things about network marketing is that we can tailor it to suit anyone. It is truly a universal business that can fit around anyone's schedule. Let your prospects know that you care by asking them about themselves. One question, if it is the right one, can often make the difference between winning or losing the prospect. What it boils down to is that you have to ask them what they want and then offer them that very thing. You are not being deceptive. Network marketing can give people whatever they want from life, no matter what that is. They have never had an opportunity like this before and probably never will again.

Most people you will meet have already put in enough effort to be independently wealthy, but effort alone is not enough. The effort has to be put into the right business – in our case the business of network marketing.

Find dissatisfied successfuls

You are looking for people who are dissatisfied with their income or their lifestyle, but you are not looking for just anybody. True, anybody can become successful at network marketing, but it is only logical that really exceptional individuals will tend to be far more successful than those who are only average to start with. Out of every hundred people – and remember you will have at least 100 on your prospect list – there are one or two such exceptional individuals. On the other hand, many ordinary people can rise to the top and become exceptional, developing and growing with their business far beyond the limits of the ordinary. If you develop any such people in your group they will soon make themselves known by their boundless enthusiasm, by their native intelligence, desire to learn and stickability, and by the successful application of the principles of success until they experience their own success. The purpose of this chapter is to help you show anyone, from the ordinary prospects to the one or two exceptionals, how they personally can benefit from your business and thus hopefully to recruit them into your group.

The method is this – find out what they want and then offer that to them. For that purpose, here are some questions that you could find useful.

Q. 'How would you like to make your vocation your vacation?'

You can stress the fun side of the business to a prospect who responds well to this question. If you really enjoy your work it becomes your leisure.

Q. 'Are you getting paid what you are worth?'

Most people think they are underpaid, so the answer will usually be 'No'. You can then respond with, 'Would you like to be?'

Q. Do you get along with your boss?

If they don't, then it gives you the opportunity to say, 'Would you like to be involved in a business where everyone co-operates and there is no ill will?

Q. Have you gone as far as possible in your job?

There are few things quite as frustrating as having no possible outlet for ambition.

Q. Are you waiting for someone to die or retire before you get promotion?

The long, slow climb up the corporate ladder is a soul killer. Many people dream of escape but are trapped by their situation. You can offer them that escape.

Q. Could you handle more challenge in your career?

There is no doubt that network marketing holds great challenge for everyone involved.

Q. Would you like to make better money and have better tax deductions?

The financial rewards are limited only by the effort that is contributed. As a self-employed distributor, you can deduct more expenses than an employed person.

Q. What would your response be if someone offered you an enjoyable career with unlimited earnings potential?

If someone says, 'I wouldn't be interested', then don't waste any more time on them. If they offer a positive response then it gives you an opening.

Q. How important is financial independence to you?

By financial independence we mean sufficiently financially secure to be able to live on the interest of our savings. Most people will never be financially independent working for someone else and I've never met anyone yet who would not like to be.

Q. If I gave you a post-dated cheque for £1,000,000 payable in five years, a five-year contract and a job description within your capabilities, would you be willing to work thirty to forty hours a week for it?

That is what a contract with a network marketing company is worth. The job description is simple. Sell the product regularly, recruit one person a month and teach them to do what you are doing. It is so simple that it is unbelievable. It is so unbelievable that most people won't do it.

Q. Would you be interested in an opportunity to really enhance your personal confidence and development?

People really grow in this business. They gradually come out of their shells and turn into the leaders that they have to be to achieve success. One of my great personal pleasures is watching this development as it happens. That is what I call job satisfaction.

Q. Have you ever had a dream of achieving something better than the everyday working life of the ordinary businessperson?

We are looking for dreamers but not day-dreamers. We are the dream workers!

Q. Would you be prepared to change some of your habits to achieve your aims in life?

I've asked this question hundreds of times and rarely got 'No' as the answer. The only people who would answer 'No' are the same people who would answer no to the question, 'Would you like to know something to your advantage?', and they are not worth worrying about.

Q. Would you be interested in developing a secondary income far exceeding what you now earn without quitting your job?

Most people start on a part-time basis and then, when they see their part-time income beginning to exceed their full-time income, they go full time.

Q. If you had a desert island and you knew for a fact that there was buried treasure somewhere on it, how long would you keep hunting for it?

Success is the hidden treasure in the island of network marketing. You even have the advantage of someone pointing to it and say-ing, *'There it is. Do what you have to do and go and get it.'* There is no mystery. There is no secret formula. There are no short cuts. Recruit and sell, it is as simple as that.

Now write out twenty questions of your own to use!

Fact: Most people stay in their existing jobs by being mediocre or by buckling under to those further up the ladder. If they were brilliant at their jobs they would be a threat to those above them. If they didn't buckle under, even when clearly in the right, they would be fired. You can give them the chance to assert their own personalities.

Moulding to Fit

Let's take a look now at how we can tailor this business to suit anybody. We will examine a conversation between Jane, who is already involved, and Bill, who is not, as they meet for coffee. For the purposes of the conversation we will imagine that Jane and Bill are not close friends.

Jane: **How are you getting on Bill?**

Bill: Not too bad. Business is a bit slow just now but it is like that for everyone.

Jane: **I know it is like that for a lot of people.**

Bill: It's the recession.

Jane: **Do you find you have a problem with any particular aspect of your business or is it just slow all over?**

Bill: Well, now that I think about it, trying to get money in on time is the main problem. I'm sick of having to wait ninety days for payments.

Jane: **I know how you feel. Listen, what would you say if I told you that I've come across a business that has a positive cashflow where everybody pays up front?**

Bill: Tell me more.

Jane: **Look, I'm not an expert because I've only just got involved. But I know a man who is. He is actually looking for**

61

some more people to help expand the business in this area. How would you like to meet him?

Bill: What is it all about?

Jane: I wouldn't know where to even start but, as I said, there is an expert on the business coming to this area soon. What is the next evening that you have free?

Notice that Jane gives Bill the choice of choosing the date. He is bound to be free some time so there is no way he can avoid it.

The astute reader will have noticed by now that a key to success in this business is not to say too much on your first approach.

By all means tell everyone you meet about the business but don't tell them much. Just tell them enough to get them curious.

The difference maker!

If you get into a conversation with someone and he asks what you do, just say, 'I make the difference'.

He is bound to say, 'What do you make the difference to?' So bounce it back at him, 'Is there anything in your life that you'd like to change?'

Few people are entirely satisfied with their lot, so by introducing the business to them you can do them more good than a Fairy Godmother. You are not limited to three wishes. More money? More freedom? More free time? More friends? More respect? More success? Freedom from stress? To travel the world?

You have the power to grant all their wishes provided they will do what it takes. You could even use the Fairy Godmother approach with a suitable prospect: 'If I could grant you three wishes, what would they be?' Whatever they ask for, say 'Granted', and invite them to a briefing where they will find out how to get those wishes.

Objections

One of the most difficult objections to deal with is when someone tells you they have 'no free time'.

You will find that a lot of potential prospects use this as a reason not to get involved. It is your job to find out if it is genuine or if they are just looking for an excuse. If they are looking for a way out, then don't stand in their way by trying to persuade them otherwise. There are enough enthusiastic, highly motivated people out there just waiting to be found. Don't waste your valuable time with no-hopers. I tell you this from experience, because I've done it – if you do persuade unsuitable people into your business, you will have to chase them all the time to get any work done. As soon as you let them out on their own, they will start to fade away. They won't phone you. They will fail to turn up to trainings and meetings, and they will drain you of your time and energy to little avail. If you have prospects who are really interested, but just can't see a way into the business because they believe they have no free time, there is a chance that you could show them otherwise.

Very rarely do you meet anyone who genuinely has no free time. Most people waste some of their time each day and if they take a hard look at this business then they are going to see that it is worth their while to free some of this time to make money. What we hope will happen is that, as the time they devote to this business pays off exceptionally well compared to the other things they are doing, they will give network marketing more and more of their time.

Over 95 per cent of the people involved in network marketing start on a part-time basis. Almost all who are exceptionally successful – that is about one person in 250 – are involved full time. So you can see that not all who are involved full time are exceptionally successful. The reason is not difficult to discover – they don't do what it takes. They treat the business like a normal job, working nine to five with perhaps the odd evening at a training or a briefing. As you should have gathered by now, that's not the way to riches.

**Maxim: For exceptional success you have to
work exceptionally hard.**

Another objection that crops up continually is, 'It wouldn't work here'. The best way to get around this one is to pre-empt the question with the information that the business is up and running, and working successfully in the area in question – if it is. They can't possibly then say, 'It wouldn't work here'.

Pyramid selling

Of all the objections that occur, one that occurs most commonly is 'network marketing is the same as pyramid selling'.

This is an easy objection to counter. Pyramid selling was a 1960s' phenomenon which was outlawed. It worked in the following way:

- a large amount of stock would be purchased by one person;

- that person would split the stock into a number of packages and sell it off at a large profit.

Each of those purchasers would then do the same, putting up the price to give them a large profit.

The process would then be repeated a number of times until the stock was unsaleable because of the escalating price.

Those at the bottom of the pyramid were often left with garages full of this useless stock.

Such schemes all had a number of things in common:

- there was no end user of the stock;

- the stock was often unsaleable in the first place;

- the whole process was unsustainable, and ended in collapse and police investigations.

Compare this type of operation with that of the modern-day network marketing company with many years of networking experience, massive turnover of stock, huge networks of distributors from all walks of life, including consumer protection officers, debt-free operation and the financial stability of major banking institutions.

Key phrases to remember and use

- I think I've found something interesting.

- We could be looking for someone else who wants to earn a bit of extra cash.

- Meet me for a coffee.

- I need a bit of help to investigate this business.

- We are developing a number of secondary profit centres.

- I make the difference.

- If it's to be, it's up to me.

- Say a little to a lot.

- Do it now!

IN BRIEF

This chapter has shown you:

- **how to find out what people want in order to offer them that very thing**

- **how to use the 'Fairy Godmother' approach**

- **how to mould the business to suit anyone**

- **how to make the difference**

- **how to cope with objections.**

NOTES, IDEAS AND THINGS TO DO

— 6 —

THROUGH THE CHANGES

A 'make over' is a complete change of external appearance from the hair down. When I started in the network marketing business I underwent such a drastic change in my appearance that my wife thought I was having an affair. You may not need such a drastic make over if you already look like a successful businessperson in top physical condition with no bad habits, but even then there are going to have to be *some* changes in everything from your personal hygiene to your attitude. Not willing to do that? Then you are wasting your time reading this book because you don't have enough commitment to succeed. Willing? Then read on.

The changes

1. Hygiene

Personal hygiene is very important to your success. First impressions really do count. Would you enjoy doing business with someone who looked as though they were in need of a shower? Neither would I! If you are guilty of not showering as often as you should, wearing the same socks or underwear two days in a row, not changing your shirt as often as you should, or the less obvious to you, but more obvious to others, schoolboy/girl offences such as not cleaning your ears, not washing your neck or hair every day, then now is the time to change that habit.

This business will change your whole life if you let it, but some things you have to change on your own. Start now. Shower every morning without fail. If it is a hot day, don't skip the shower when you get home, no matter how tired you are.

When you go to a briefing you should have a glowing, healthy look. Men – if you have a heavy growth of beard, shave immediately before you go. Use a moisturised aftershave for that extra shine. Use a good conditioner on your hair. Women should get a good beautician to show them how to apply the minimum make-up to suit their face.

2. Fitness

Take a good look at yourself in the mirror. Is your body out of condition? Do you think that a pot belly projects an image of success? Could it be time to establish that exercise regime that you have always been promising yourself to do? Jane Fonda has an excellent cure for pot bellies. If you can't cope with aerobics then take up swimming or squash. A lot of successful people attend squash clubs. Many of them are potentially successful distributors, but they don't yet know this because you haven't told them.

Join a good health club and make full use of the facilities. Do you really want to relax? Have a work out, a sauna, a Jacuzzi and a really good massage. That should relieve all your tensions. It'll turn you to jelly, but you will be relaxed.

3. Healthy diet

You can't be successful if you are lying on your back ill. Since prevention is better than cure, it is time to change all those unhealthy eating habits. The healthiest of all is a vegetarian diet – hence research shows that vegetarians live five years longer on average than meat eaters. They also enjoy a better quality of life, being less prone to all forms of cancer, heart disease, diabetes, liver and kidney problems and strokes. If you can't bring yourself to give up meat altogether, then you should seriously consider at least giving up red meat.

How many drinks do you have a week? More than two a night is too many. You need a clear head to make good decisions. Have a fling now and then by all means but stay sober as a rule. If you can 'handle your drink', then your body has become accustomed to it because you are drinking too much. Seek help if you have a problem in this area. Don't make excuses like, 'I'm not addicted, I do it because I enjoy it'.

4. Accident avoidance

Tragically, a number of very successful distributors are lost every year through road accidents. Most of them are driving very expensive cars capable of travelling at more than double the speed limit. If one of your habits is driving too fast then change that habit and help ensure that you stay around long enough to enjoy spending all the money that you are going to be making. You'll save a lot of petrol too.

4. Smoking – *don't*

If you have the will-power to give up smoking then you have the will-power to succeed in network marketing. Can you do it for a day? If so then that is enough. One day, then one day, then one day . . . Besides, your breath will smell sweeter, you'll save money, you'll improve your health and you won't display the addiction – essentially a weakness – in front of potential distributors.

5. Develop a winning attitude

Network marketing is 10 per cent knowledge and 90 per cent attitude. If you have the right attitude, no matter how little you know about the business, then your enthusiasm will be infectious and success will follow. On the other hand, if you have the wrong attitude then no matter how much you know, your business will fail. 'So what' I hear you ask, 'is the right attitude?'

At a training in Inverness, Scotland, where I was invited to give a talk on sales success, I was interested to hear another trainer, Dave Penney, quoting a little phrase that struck me as very true:

> **People don't care how much you know until they
> know how much you care.**

If you don't love people and love working with people then network marketing is not for you. You have to care about each and every member of your group. You succeed by helping others achieve success. If you are selfishly interested in profiting from your group rather than helping them make their profit, then you will fail. If a member of your group asks you to come and help, no matter where that person is in the country, you should put time aside to provide the help.

Perhaps when you signed on, your sponsor was selfish, didn't spend time with you and you've had to learn the hard way. If that is the case it is a wonder you have survived. Don't treat your distributors the same way if you want to build successfully. They are unlikely to be so lucky.

A warm smile can make the difference between your success and failure. Try it now. Smile even if you don't feel like smiling. It is difficult to feel depressed with a smile on your face. This is a subject I will return to later, but you should begin right now. Smiling must become such a habit to you that people will look forward to meeting you because of your happy attitude to life and, as you draw people to you, you will become more successful and really have something to smile about.

The personal confidence that you exude will have a great influence on your credibility. If you lack self-confidence you will have difficulty getting people to respect you and believe you. Read Chapter 21 to help you in this area.

The most important attitude that you can have is a professional attitude. With this you can attract professional quality people. Without it you will have great difficulty getting them to join your business.

If you are wondering how you can be expected to smile all the time and still have a professional attitude, then you are right. There comes a time when you have to be serious. Cultivate a good 'bedside' manner. When you are talking business you should have the knowledge and professional attitude equal to that of an accountant or bank manager. You may not be up to that yet, but if you work through this book and follow the programme of personal development which is between these covers, you will one day be able to impress any level of management.

6. Developing a balanced character

A well-balanced character is a prime requisite for success. If you answer yes to any of the questions below, then you will have to tackle the problem at its roots. Chapter 12, on creative thinking and problem solving, can help you do this. If you answer any of the questions untruthfully then you are only deceiving yourself at painful cost to your long-term development.

Do you find it difficult to relax?

There are classes available on relaxation in many towns and cities. Ask at your local library for information on local classes. Alternatively, if you attend an exercise class there will usually be a relaxation period after the exercises are over. Thus, you can get fit and learn to relax properly at the same time. A number of other solutions are possible. You could use an aerobics video, since there is always a warm-up period before the exercises and a well-planned relaxation period after them.

Yoga or meditation classes are an alternative to aerobics, and can really help you to get to know yourself and to sort out any problems that you have. After all, the solution to most of your problems is within yourself. It is just a matter of finding them. Do not be put off by the word 'meditation'. The methods are simple and have the advantage that it is impossible to meditate properly when you are tense.

If you want to try meditation, simply go to a quiet room, get into a comfortable position, preferably sitting upright to prevent you from falling asleep, and close your eyes. Consciously relax your body starting at your feet, using a sort of self-hypnosis which simply means telling your body what to do. For example, 'My feet are warm, comfortable and totally relaxed. My calves are warm and totally relaxed . . .' etc. and work your way up until your whole body is relaxed.

Once you have achieved relaxation, the next stage is to concentrate on your breathing. The purpose of this is to control your mind. When you are concentrating on breathing your mind is not skipping about from one problem to the next, so it gets a well-earned rest. Simply allow yourself to be aware of your breath entering and leaving your nostrils, and of your chest rising and falling. This method of beginning meditation is so simple, yet so powerful that many people feel an almost mystical self-awareness and peace of mind after only a short period of practice. If you become particularly interested in meditation, you will find details of books on the subject in the list of recommended reading at the back of this book.

Do you ever fly into a temper?

Self-control can be difficult for those under stress, but you lose respect when you lose your temper. Remember the line from Rudyard Kipling's poem, 'If':

> If you can keep your head when all about you
> Are losing theirs and blaming it on you . . .

An even temper is an important asset to the successful distributor. Network marketing can often be the most frustrating business in the world, with people letting you down, breaking promises, failing to turn up at meetings and generally doing their best to drive you up the wall. Try to be like Robert Burns's man of independent mind who 'looks and laughs at a' that'.

Are you troubled by your conscience?

We have all done things that we regret in the past. Face up to the fact that there is no way that you can change what has already happened. But there is a way to ease your conscience. You can make amends. If you have wronged someone, then do right by them now and do far more than you have to. There are skeletons in everyone's cupboard. Perhaps you have hurt someone you love? Let them know that you realise you hurt them and that you are sorry. Now, go really out of your way to prove that you love them. Make that person feel good and you will feel good.

Perhaps you have hurt someone who has died and it is impossible to make personal amends to them? Then make amends by doing good with your life in the knowledge that the person you hurt would approve. Choose a charity to help, and devote quality *time* and money to help it. I stress the word time because you can't buy yourself a clear conscience. You have to do something that involves investing time – your most valuable asset – to help others.

Do you have trouble sleeping?

Many have fallen into the trap of dependency on pills to help them sleep, but in the long run pills often do more harm than good. If this is the case for you, take your doctor's advice on weaning yourself off the pills and start to use natural techniques to get to sleep. Read a chapter of a book, use self-hypnosis, listen to Bing Crosby, drink a soothing herbal tea or whatever turns you off. On the subject of tea and coffee, perhaps you should try cutting down on the amount you consume. Caffeine in your blood not only keeps you awake, but is an addictive drug which has other more subtle effects on the body. Long-term studies on members of the Mormon faith (who abstain from tea, coffee and alcohol) have shown that, like vegetarians, on average they live five years longer than other people from the same population group. I am not suggesting that you follow their example, but perhaps you could make more use of herbal teas and decaffeinated coffee.

Are you afraid to face any aspect of your life?

Take a good, hard look at yourself. What exactly are you afraid of? Write it down and you will begin to take control of it. Perhaps you are trapped in an unhappy relationship that is getting worse and worse, but you are afraid to leave? When you write down what is wrong you will begin to see the reality of the situation more clearly and be better able to decide what to do.

Perhaps you are trapped in the situation of having massive debts, with no easy way out? It is unlikely that network marketing is going to work fast enough for you to solve these problems. It would be far better to get a solution sorted out now, even if it involves bankruptcy. There are debt counsellors with every Citizens' Advice Bureau who should be able to help. The important thing to realise is that tackling your problem can only improve your situation.

Fear is a symptom of insecurity. As you begin to make a success of your life through network marketing, you will grow in personal confidence and your insecurity will disappear. Start to do what it takes and your situation, no matter how bad it is, can only improve. When you are down, the only way to go is up.

Do you spend too much time day-dreaming?

If this is the case then you are probably highly creative, but have never found a proper outlet for your creativity. Now is the time to change all that. Do you enjoy writing? Join a local writers' group. If there isn't one in your area then start one up. If you are musically inclined, perhaps you should take lessons and join or form a local musical group or band. There are many other outlets for creativity. You could attend an evening class at your local college and learn to paint or sculpt. The possibilities are endless and infinitely more worthwhile than daydreaming. Doing is better than dreaming.

Do you ever get violent?

When you lash out in violence you often hurt yourself as much as the person you strike. If you cannot control this aspect of your life, then you should seek immediate professional help. Violent behaviour can lose you everything you have worked so hard to achieve. You may hide it from the world and achieve wealth, but if you are violent you can never truly be happy.

When a person is violent there are usually strong emotional forces at work in their psyche. There can be influences from an unhappy or violent childhood, from failed relationships, from loss of love and from the general frustrations of life. Sharing your problems with a trained counsellor can help you to come to grips with the thing that is causing the problems you are having. Face up to it now and do something about it.

Do you get depressed for long periods?

Apart from the various hormonal or medical causes of depression, which can be treated by hormone replacement, or by drug or vitamin therapy, depression is usually a symptom of an unhappy lifestyle. Many people do not realise that they are in control of their own lives and what happens to them. It is up to you what you do with your life. The rest of your life starts right now. In the process of working through this book you will effect many changes on your life and your personality, but only if you really do it instead of just reading about it. This book is about bringing you fortune and happiness. You can't be depressed and happy at the same time, so your problem will soon cease to exist.

-7-

FOCUSING IN ON

YOUR MARKET

Your first sixty to ninety days in network marketing, as in any self-employed sales business, will be the most difficult. On your initial prospect list there are bound to be a fair number of names who are not interested in the product line that your company offers. After all, the list is a totally random selection of people you know. You have to gradually make your way towards a prospect list of people who are interested. Take for example diet biscuits. If your prospects are not on a diet then they won't buy, but if you get referrals from them then they are likely to point you in the direction of people they know who are on diets, so you have focused in a bit.

When you go to the referrals you will find that they are closer to your target market and – still with the diet biscuits example – being of the overweight persuasion, they will know others like themselves. They may be members of a slimming club. They may know of other clubs in the slimming or keep fit line. When you get to the club members I think you will agree that you are right on your target market. If you can't sell diet biscuits to these people then you are doing something wrong. Chapter 8 should help you.

The same principle goes for any of the products that are sold through network marketing. Take water filters as another example. Many of your prospect list may be completely satisfied with the water they already have, even if it tastes terrible. You know that your filter unit vastly improves the taste of the water, but you can't sell to everybody. However, even those you don't sell to should be able to point you in the right direction. Those people who are into diets and keep fit are also into healthy food and drink, so by coincidence you are looking for a similar target market to the diet biscuit salesperson. Clearly with water filters you are not restricted to health food addicts, but they are a good starting point for you and they will know other people who are into a healthy lifestyle.

Hit the target!

Most people have some area of knowledge or expertise that could suggest to them the type of product they should be concentrating on. A plumber, for example would be the ideal candidate for selling water filters. Plumbers are in and out of people's houses all the time dealing with water fittings. How simple it would be to suggest that the quality of drinking water at a house could really be improved by fitting a filter under the sink. So, if you are not a plumber yourself, and you are selling water filters, what about bringing some plumbers into your team?

No matter what product you are selling, you can make good use of the people-gathering properties of clubs and organisations, especially if you are a member. I know of one distributor who makes almost all of his contacts on the golf course and he runs a very successful business. A lot of people envy the life he leads, playing golf every afternoon and closing contracts in the clubhouse afterwards.

The secret of his success? He uses the golf clubs he sells, he is a great player and he is very modest. He travels all over the country playing, but he puts his success down to his golf clubs. In short, he has narrowed down to his true market.

It is not so much who *you* know as who those people know. Get the right people into your team to sell for you. When they sell to all of their specialist contacts, they will make you a lot of money in the process.

Who would be the ideal candidate to sell naughty undies, do you think? What about the average housewife, with a mischievous sense of humour?

Find the right person

To sell books, a librarian would have a good circle of contacts. If you are selling children's books, use schools and playschools. Headteachers are always looking for ways to raise funds for their school. Offer discounts and rebates for bulk purchases. Perhaps you could suggest that the headteacher becomes a distributor – 'to ease paperwork'. Invite the teacher out for a meal to discuss the matter. It is worth spending time with quality prospects who are in your true target market.

If you are selling perfume and cosmetics use women's guilds to find contacts. One free sample bottle can sell twenty or more. During an evaluation of a new line for my company, my own mother sold fifty products over two guild meetings, making a considerable profit for the guild in the process.

If you are selling high-quality chess boards then use chess clubs. Take one up around the clubs and demonstrate it. Each chess player will know of a number of others who could be interested. Or better still, recruit keen chess players as distributors.

Trade Fairs

Take a look through your local newspaper's diary. Find when trade fairs, county shows and gala days are on and make sure that you book a stall.

The trick to using trade fairs successfully is to get really well organised.

1. Get a pretty girl to help you on the stall and you should double your enquiries from men. Get a handsome young man and see how many more women you attract.

2. Have your stall brightly coloured and well decorated. You should be able to get posters and literature from your company to decorate the area of your stall.

3. Have a video running at your stall. Even running on a loop it draws customers like a magnet.

4. Give away free samples of your product if possible. Have a big sign saying 'FREE'.

5. Get relatives and friends to come clustering round your stall. It is amazing how others will be attracted to the stall. People act strangely like sheep sometimes.

6. Run a free-to-enter raffle, competition or prize draw, the winner gets a free product or other prize. Each name entered for the raffle gets a free home demonstration of the product. By the end of a successful day you should have at least twenty demonstrations for each person present at the stall.

7. Give away free badges about your company or product with the offer of a free demo and your phone number.

8. Children can pull parents towards your stall, so make sure you have free balloons or other gifts on display and aimed specially at them. But don't waste the chance to advertise your company and product on the free gifts.

Demonstration stock

There are other ways to get your demonstration stock to the public eye. If your product is suitable – for example, recirculatory air purifiers, you can leave demonstration units with local doctors, dentists and hairdressers on a free trial basis. Put a label on the units saying something like:

> **EXCELLENT FOR ASTHMA AND HAY FEVER**
> **SUFFERERS. IF YOU ENJOY BREATHING THE CLEAN,**
> **FRESH AIR FROM THIS UNIT PLEASE CONTACT** _____
> **ON TEL. NO** _____ **FOR A FREE HOME TRIAL.**

Do be careful about claims that you make for the medical properties of products. Your company may even forbid such claims. However, it is unlikely that a potential customer will object to your wording. If they do, there is one way for them to find out if the product will help them – try it out, free of charge!

You can take this approach a step further by paying for referrals that lead to sales. If the hairdresser points the unit out to customers, mentioning the benefits, and the customer after a free trial decides to take one of your units, then you can pay the hairdresser a proportion of your profit. The more you pay, the more enthusiastic the hairdresser will be about your unit. I know of one particular distributor who makes a good living using this approach alone. He also has the smartest haircuts you've ever seen.

A dentist friend of mine who unfortunately is not in my downline, has the perfect opportunity to sell to a 'captive' market. Would you say 'no' to someone who is hovering over you with a high speed drill? Frankly, he sold to me when I was still in the waiting room!

I have another friend who sells high pressure cleaners. To whom do you think he sells them? I'll give you a clue – they work with dirt. He sells to farmers. Believe it or not, he spent two years trying to sell them to garages before he found his true market. 'Ah,' I hear you saying, 'he should be able to sell them to garages.' The trouble is that every other high pressure cleaner salesperson in the country is trying to sell to garages. So my friend spends a lot more on petrol, but he sells more alone than any other two salespeople in the company.

Don't stop looking. There are people who want what you sell. In fact they are desperate for your problem-solving product. The fact is that most people give up before they have even found their true market.

Now that would be a foolish thing to do, wouldn't it?

IN BRIEF

This chapter has shown you:

- **how to find your true market**
- **which is the most difficult period**
- **how to use club contacts**
- **how to use trade fairs to make contacts**
- **the use of customer referrals**
- **how to use demonstration stock to get orders.**

NOTES, IDEAS AND THINGS TO DO

– 8 –

SALES

In many ways this is the most important aspect of the whole business. Network marketing is the fastest way of moving product directly from the manufacturer to the end user. There is no way around it; the foundation of a solid business must rest on retail sales, otherwise you will have little better than a pyramid-selling operation that will fall down about your ears.

Positive thinking is the key to success in network marketing, including the sales aspect. Before you go on your sales call you have to get into the right frame of mind. Listen to inspirational tapes. Focus in on your aims. How are you going to achieve them? By selling, that's how. Selling the business, selling the product and, most of all, selling yourself. Read through your maxims. Maximise your potential. You have to be buzzing with energy and personal magnetism before you go out.

The ideal product is something nobody has, everybody wants and everybody can afford. If you can find something with such universal appeal then you have a winner. All you have to do is allow the customers to find out what you have and they will buy it. Your first customers will be the names on your prospect lists who are not going to be approached with the business, although some of the people whom you do introduce to the business concepts will also order the product.

If you have previous sales experience, much of what you already know can help you, but don't count on it. If you are a master of the hard sell then you are going to have a lot of relearning to do. A lot of your success in this business will depend on getting good referrals from customers. If you try to do a hard sell you will get no referrals and possibly no sale.

Making the sales appointments

The principle is the same as when making appointments to meet business prospects. Don't tell them details about the business or the products. Just get the appointment. Here are a few suggested scripts which you can adapt for your own use:

> *John:* **Hi Anne, John here. Listen, I've started up a little business of my own and I'd like to show you what I've got. Can I pop round tonight and show you it?**
>
> *Anne:* What is it that you have?
>
> *John:* **I'd rather you judged it when I get there. Is that OK?**

If Anne really insists that you tell her all about the product over the phone just say: 'Sorry Anne, I have to go now. I'll call you some other time. Cheerio.'

Then just hang up. When you do call back, perhaps in a few weeks, she may be curious.

Another script:

> *John:* **Hi Anne, John here. Do you have five minutes? I'd like to pop round and show you something.**
>
> *Anne:* Show me what?
>
> *John:* **I'll tell you when I get there.**

Another approach is just to call the number and if anyone answers then hang up and go straight round.

Plan your schedule properly so that you are not running backwards and forwards from different areas.

In the Door

When you are in the door get straight down to business. Try and get the husband and wife together. You need them both to make the decision to buy. We will use the example of our imaginary everlasting lightbulbs (ELB) again.

Straight away get the prospects involved. Get the husband or wife to plug in a bulb and demonstrate the high quality of the light. Then play the company's short promotional video. If it is well produced it should do the hardest part of the sale for you. If you have no video then go into your prepared sales pitch telling how the ELBs are on special offer – if they are.

You should emphasise the benefits such as their unique ability to repel insects and point out the long-term savings before allowing the subject of cost to crop up.

Never mention the word 'buy' or 'purchase'. If they do ask the price prematurely, just say, 'I'll be coming to that soon.'

After your presentation comes the wonderful moment when you have to ask for the sale. There are many ways to broach this delicate subject. I suggest that you do it gently using the step-by-step question approach, posing the questions in such a way that they have no option but to say 'Yes' to most of them – unless they are going to be deliberately awkward to spite you.

- Did you enjoy the demonstration?

- Do you like the quality of light that the units provide?

- Do you realise that because of their low electricity consumption, they pay for themselves within a year?

- Do you realise that if you have these ELBs installed you will never have to buy another lightbulb or flyspray?

- Do you think that the model with the built-in infra-red heater is useful for the toilet?

- Do you like the combined fire alarm units?

And for the final question look them right in the eye and ask:

From your reaction I can tell that you really like these

everlasting bulbs. Would you like to own some of them for yourself?

And don't take your eyes off them until they answer.

They have answered all your questions 'Yes' so far, so if the answer to this one is 'No', don't be discouraged immediately. Find out why not. If they simply can't afford them perhaps you can offer them the 'One-a-Month' deal that the company has or the hire purchase scheme.

Handling sales objections

If the customer has only one objection then you have made the sale when you get round it. Ask the question, 'Is that your only objection?' Perhaps their single objection is that they think the bulbs are too bright. Offer the lower wattage. Now they have to buy.

By far the best way to handle a sales objection is to turn it to your advantage.

If the customer asks you something like, 'Do these everlasting light bulbs kill dragonflies?' just bounce it back at the customer.

Ask them, 'Do you have that problem?'

The chances are that they don't. Alternatively, you may have a suitable product and can ask them, in a suitably dejected voice, 'Are you looking for lightbulbs that do kill dragonflies?'

If they answer 'Yes', and you can offer them a suitable product, then they can hardly say 'No'. The important thing is that they arrive at the decision to purchase as a result of choices they have taken rather than as a result of pressure.

It is sometimes possible to avoid getting a 'No' by just reaching the decision that they have decided to buy on your own and saying something like, 'Great. Will I plug them in, or do you want to do that yourself?'

Or similarly, 'Great. Let's get the paperwork over with.'

Note that you haven't asked the final question, 'Would you like to own these units?' You don't need to ask that with this approach. This is a good way to handle customers who just can't seem to come to a decision on their own, but it goes a bit against the grain of 'no pressure'.

It depends which approach you are most comfortable with.

Incentives

If the customer comes up with the answer, 'I'd like to think about it', then offer an incentive to close the deal. Tell them that you have a free gift to offer if they decide tonight. Always keep a bottle of wine in the car for this purpose. If the deal is large enough you can offer them a crate of wine. Pick a good but cheap wine from a supermarket. A crate of wine sounds like a substantial free gift, but you should be able to pick one up for a small proportion of your profit on the deal.

Good incentives: wine; tickets to local night club; tickets to sauna or health club; free food voucher (you can easily arrange to purchase these from most supermarkets); food hampers; free product; free prerecorded video or music CD; immediate discount. I know of one magic-fingered distributor who offers a free massage.

Humour

Use your imagination and creativity. Develop and use your sense of humour. If you get the prospects laughing with you then you have done the hardest part of the sale – making the prospect like you. First and foremost you are selling yourself. Tune in to the customers. Find out what they like and use that information to establish a rapport. People buy for lots of reasons, but if they don't like you they are unlikely to buy from you. It is your primary task to make the customer like you. A sense of humour is the most important tool you can take with you on a sales call. If you can laugh at yourself, laugh at your problems, laugh at failure, laugh at rejection, laugh at arrogance, laugh at stupidity, laugh at discouragement, laugh at cold feet and wet hair, laugh at slammed doors, laugh at weeks of hard slog with little or no success, and keep on laughing at it for weeks and months on end then you have what it takes to become a network marketing millionaire.

TRY IT – YOU'LL LIKE IT!

As previously mentioned, there is another approach to retailing which has given certain companies phenomenal growth. This is the 'Try It – You'll Like It' approach. If your company's product is suitable then you can leave it with the customer for a few days to allow them to try it out. The Unsolicited Goods Act does not apply here, as you are leaving the goods at the request of the customer. If the product is as good as you claim, and provides real benefits, then you shouldn't be afraid to try this approach. When you go back on your return call, which should be at a time arranged with the customer on your first visit, it will be immediately clear if they are interested in owning your product. If the answer is a *definite* 'No', then my advice is don't try to persuade them otherwise. You will spoil your chances of getting referrals.

Very occasionally you may have trouble getting back goods which you have left on approval when the customer wants the product, but simply doesn't want to pay. I favour personal visits to such customers by the salesman who left the product there. I've never known a personal visit to fail either to recover the goods or to make the sale.

Expect the sale

Generally you will get what you expect to get from life and from your customers. If you go into their house expecting them to say 'No' then that is almost certainly what they will say. On the other hand, if you are full of expectation of the sale, tensed up and just waiting for the word 'Yes', with an eager look on your face, the customer is less likely to say 'No'. It is human nature not to want to hurt people. They are going to look at your face and say, 'Oh my God, look at his face, he is so eager. I can't possibly disappoint him.' I learnt this from a young saleswoman who sold encyclopedias to me and just about everyone else in our street. She knew very little about the encyclopedias, but she didn't have to – she just showed them and they were good. She knew very little

about sales technique, but she didn't have to. She was just so
eager that it was simply a pleasure to say 'Yes' to her in order not
to see a look of devastating disappointment on her young face.

Referrals

Never leave the customer's house without asking for referrals.
How you ask is as important as what you ask. It is no use saying,
'Do you know anyone who would be interested in a little demo of
these products?' If you do try this question, the customer will
usually think for a moment and say, 'No, sorry.'

You have to approach the subject in a whole different way.
Before you go simply ask them to fetch their address or phone
number book so that you can put your details in it. When you
write them in, hand the book back and give the customer a referral
card asking simply, 'Could you put a few names and addresses
down here for me please? We only work from personal recom-
mendations.'

Since the customer has the address book already at hand, you
are in with a good chance. If the customer refuses then just laugh
and say, 'Well don't worry, you're not alone. Another customer
refused to give me referrals last week but I eventually caught up
with things again.'

The Columbo question

Remember the TV detective Columbo? When he visits a suspect
he has a unique way of solving cases by asking one key question
with his foot half out of the door. The same technique is used in
our business. After the sales visit is over, with your referrals in
your folder, having said 'Cheerio', suddenly stop and say, as an
afterthought, 'Incidentally, we are looking for some more distributors in this area. There is good money to be earned for just a few
hours' work every week. Would you happen to know anyone who
may be interested?'

If you have done your job properly, made your demonstration
really good fun for them, made the whole visit duplicatable by

keeping it simple and planted a few seeds in the right place, then the idea may pop into their heads that they could do the business themselves. Failing that, they may recommend a son, daughter, neighbour or friend. If they do, and you get a successful new distributor as a result, you will end up making far more profit than a retail sale could have made you. That is why, come what may, you should never pressure a customer into a sale. Sure – you *will* have used psychology on them, but that is simply helping the customer to realise that they want the product you are selling.

IN BRIEF

This chapter has shown you:

- **how to make the sales appointment**
- **how to demonstrate the product**
- **how to handle sales objections**
- **how to provide incentives**
- **the importance of humour**
- **the 'Try It' – 'You'll Like It' approach**
- **how to get referrals**
- **how to expect the sale**
- **how to use the 'Columbo' question.**

Notes, Ideas and Things to Do

– 9 –

LETTER AND VIDEO

PROSPECTING

This chapter is concerned with finding new members for your team rather than selling your product by mail order, although if your product is suitable, I hope that you exploit all the opportunities that mail order provides for low overhead sales.

Letters can be a very effective method of finding new prospects, but it is easy to make mistakes and lose people by saying the wrong things. The trick is to say just enough to get the prospect interested, but not enough to satisfy their curiosity. I have lost count of the number of times that new distributors have ignored all advice on this matter, and sent off totally unsuitable letters to all their best prospects, thus losing them.

It is pointless to try to include all the information that you have obtained through perhaps a month or longer of investigation in one letter. Try to communicate your enthusiasm for the business through a letter and you will only succeed in convincing them that you have flipped. Your letter will become little better than a mailshot and will end up where most ill-considered mailshots end their short lives – the bin.

Q: What's the difference between an effective letter and an ineffective mailshot?

A: A good letter is personally addressed and typed rather being a photocopy with a typed name or stuck-on label.

A: It is alone in the envelope rather than being accompanied by other 'flyers'.

A: It appeals to the individual as a person by mentioning a mutual interest or a mutual friend.

A: It is written on high-quality paper, with your personal letter-head, preferably with your gold-blocked company name.

A: It simply asks for a personal appointment rather than trying to persuade the prospect of the value of the opportunity.

A: It leaves the appointment date open.

A: It never mentions the word 'opportunity'.

A: It arouses curiosity without providing enough information to satisfy that curiosity.

A: It is signed personally by you *in blue ink*. This emphasises the individuality of the letter and is known to help response.

An *ineffective* mailshot is usually:

- unpersonalised;

- photocopied;

- full of wonderful promises;

- full of 'opportunity' and 'massive income potential';

- and offers things too good to be true – usually money for nothing.

To ensure that your letters are as effective as possible, get as much information as you can about the prospect before you write and use that knowledge to help you mention the particular areas of your business that could be of interest to the individual prospect. Register with a credit reference company. For a small fee you will be able to find out a surprising amount about your top prospects.

It is far better to write 100 highly effective letters than 500 totally useless letters. With a little bit of thought you can get the response which eludes most other writers.

Here is an example of a letter with pulling power suitable for a name given to you as part of your downline's prospect list:

```
                    COMPANY NAME
                              2 Money Walk
                                     Smile
                                   Benefit
     Tel. No.
                                      Date

     Mr Prospect
     Big House
     Richland


     Dear Mr Prospect

     We have a mutual friend in Stacy W .....
     who mentioned that you are a self-employed
     accountant with good local knowledge of the
     business community.

     COMPANY NAME are distributors for a multi-
     national marketing company which has plans
     to expand in Richland and I believe that we
     may be able to offer you the chance to
     profit from this expansion.

     I will be in Richland soon and would like
     to meet you to discuss this matter.

     Please telephone to make an appointment.


     Yours sincerely


     John Success
     (Director)
```

(*Points to note:* The letter is personalised. No information is given about the network marketing aspect of the business. The appointment date and time are left open.)

It is possible to get up to 30 per cent replies from this type of letter, provided you have chosen your prospects carefully. Some will write to ask for more information, in which case telephone to ask them for an appointment, explaining that you would rather discuss the matter in person. Some phone for more information themselves, in which case, as I mentioned earlier, sidetrack them and simply make the appointment. It is a lesson painfully learned by thousands of distributors that discussing details of the business with prospects over the phone is a waste of time. The concept can't be explained convincingly in a few minutes.

If a prospect refuses a meeting, you could send a video on the off-chance that they could change their mind, but it is rare for a video to 'turn around' a prospect with a closed mind.

There are any number of reasons that you can give for not giving further information over the telephone. Here are a few:

- The concepts are 90 per cent visual.

- I wouldn't do the company justice.

- I don't know enough about it yet to be able to explain it properly, but there is someone I'd like you to meet who knows much more.

- The experts can explain it far better than I can, so I wouldn't even try.

- I never discuss the business over the phone.

- Sorry, it would take too long to tell you about it over the phone.

- I'd rather discuss the business with you in person.

- I wouldn't know where to start.

- We are specially looking for people with open enough minds to come along with the information that you already have. You will find out the rest when you get there.

Here is another suggested letter – this time for 'cold' prospecting.

```
                    COMPANY NAME
                                   2 Money Walk
                                         Smile
                                        Benefit
   Tel. No.
                                           Date

   Mr Prospect
   Big House
   Richland


   Dear Mr Prospect

   I am involved with an international distri-
   bution company and we have plans to expand
   in Richland. Since you are listed as a
   self-employed draughtsman, and therefore
   have a good knowledge of your local busi-
   ness community, I believe that we can offer
   you the chance to profit from this expan-
   sion.

   I would be interested to meet you at the
   Imperial Hotel on Saturday 4 June to dis-
   cuss this matter.

   Please telephone to make an appointment.


   Yours sincerely


   John Success
   (Director)
```

(*Points to note:* A good response can be expected if you make it clear that you have done your homework.)

It is possible to get up to a 10 per cent response from this type of letter, so 100 letters can give you 10 replies.

Here is an example of an unsuccessful letter – **DON'T USE IT!**

COMPANY NAME

2 Money Walk
Smile
Benefit

Tel. No.

Date

Mr Prospect
Big House
Richland

Dear Mr Prospect

A mutual friend of ours has suggested that you may be looking for a new business opportunity at the moment. As it happens, I have a position that may be suitable for you within my company. We are looking for a number of people with leadership qualities and management experience, who are looking to earn massive incomes within the framework of a company that has a fantastic track record.

I would be interested to meet you at the Imperial Hotel on Saturday 4 June to discuss this matter.

Please telephone to make an appointment.

Yours sincerely

John Success
(Director)

A number of things are wrong with this prospecting letter. For one thing, it is deceitful – the position you are offering is not an employed position as this letter would seem to imply. And who is the mysterious mutual friend? Very few people will be taken in by this phrase unless you can name someone.

The words 'business opportunity' give the lie to the rest of the letter. And offers of massive incomes are unbelievable.

The main reason not to use this letter, however, is that it just doesn't work. I know of a distributor who spent a small fortune 'burning off' (spoiling his chances with) a very high quality list of names, using this letter. Needless to say he learned by his mistake.

If you are researching a new area try and get hold of a local trade directory. The main reason for this is that self-employed people are the best prospects as distributors: they control their own time and so can attend daytime trainings and briefings, and they will be familiar with the disciplines of book keeping and tax records. They will also be used to working on their own initiative. When you work for yourself you don't get paid for doodling or driving around. You only get paid for selling or sponsoring. Use your wits and find self-employed people to approach first. Don't waste your time by approaching the wrong people.

Mailing lists

You can buy mailing lists from some companies listing people who have responded to business opportunity adverts. Be careful here. Only use a reputable company and ensure that the lists are genuine. Another factor to remember is that some network marketing companies may not allow the use of mailing lists.

As previously mentioned, never send out unpersonalised photocopied letters to those on your mailing list. I know of one man who sent out 10,000 of these and received not one single genuine reply. They just don't work.

You can also visit the local library or council offices and ask to see the voting roll. If you do choose to go cold calling, it is always better at least to know the family's name when you knock the door.

Never make specific claims regarding earning potential. This depends on too many variables. You don't want to end up getting sued by someone who foolishly gives up their job before establishing a sufficient income to live on.

The video approach

By continually circulating your promotional videos you can ensure that you always have prospects at different stages of introduction.

Most super-successful distributors use this approach as one of the many techniques that they operate. By sending out five videos per day to those who have responded to letters and phone calls, they guard against the loss of momentum which is one of the most common causes of failure to build a high-income generating group.

When using this method, always stress the importance of having the video returned to you as soon as possible.

Always keep a few videos with you to pass out to new prospects. Network marketing is not just a job, it is a way of life. Opportunities continually present themselves for introducing new people to the concepts of the business. If you ignore those opportunities you may as well change your middle name to Mediocre.

If you go into a shop to purchase something, always ask the assistant, 'Having fun?' They will usually roll their eyes at you and say something like, 'Are you kidding?' That is your opening to say, 'That's a shame. I'm involved in a really fun business so I sympathise with people who hate their job.' Then, as an afterthought, allow your facial expression to light up and say, 'As a matter of fact I have a video here that explains all about the business if you'd like to have a look at it.'

The one-in-three rule

The one-in-three rule applies here again. It may seem ridiculous or pessimistic, but in fact it is realistic. You have to face the reality of the workload that you have to get through to become successful. Do you really want to make that million? To get one very successful distributor you have to put out over 200 videos. For every three that you put out in this way, on average, one will be interested. For every three interested, one will come to a briefing or training session. For every three who come, one will sign on. For every three who sign on, one will be successful. For every three who are successful one will be very successful. Don't let the statistics drive you mad, just keep doing what it takes. That one very succesful distributor could be worth many thousands per year to you. You need at least three of them, but you would be better with five to really make it big.

The only qualification in the case of putting out videos is that the person must undertake to watch it.

Here are some other ideal opportunities to give out videos.

- **Dinner parties** During meals you have a trapped audience.

- **Business lunches** Put punch bowls into restaurants and offer free business lunches to all who leave their cards in it. Give a presentation before they get a chance to eat and let them take videos to watch at home.

- **Taxi drivers** They have a wide range of contacts through their job and make excellent distributors.

- **Patients** If you are a vet, a doctor, a dentist, a chiropodist, an optician, a hairdresser or some kind of therapist, give your patients/clients (or their owners) a video to take home and look at. Ethics? You are doing them a favour.

When I say don't waste an opportunity I mean exactly that. If you crash your car, give a video to the driver or person that you hit, the police officers who investigate and the garage repair people who fix your vehicle.

If you fall down and break your arm, give a video to the ambulance drivers, the doctors and the nurses that you meet.

If you go to a christening or a wedding, give the guests a video.

If you visit your accountant or financial consultant, make sure that they get a video.

If the tax inspector comes to see you then show the inspector a video or send him or her away with one. Look at this conversation.

Taxman: **Where did this receipt appear from?**

Self: I was down visiting someone about this incredible business opportunity that I've discovered. How about taking a look at this video just to familiarise yourself with my business?

Taxman: **What was this cheque for?**

Self: A commission cheque for a single sale. If you would just plant yourself there, then I will put this video on.

Taxman: **Why is your income so much higher this year than in any previous year?**

Self: Shh. Watch this video and you will find out.

If you are going somewhere and you suspect that there will not be a video player available, take your own.

Keep a careful log of all your videos. Each one is an employee out there recruiting for you. Plan to succeed right from the start by getting as many as you can afford up to about fifty. Don't get caught in the trap of spending all your money on stock and leaving nothing for videos. Beware of sponsors who advise you to do that. The chances are that they are looking to short-term rebates for themselves, rather than helping you to build a long-term successful network.

Audios

You can treat audio-cassettes in exactly the same way as videos, with the added advantage that they are compact and it is easy always to have a few in your pockets. They are less effective in recruiting but cheaper, so you should be able to afford more of them.

Books

Network marketing books make excellent Christmas and birthday presents, and are a good way of letting relatives and close friends know about the business without being too pushy. In the process of reading they will gradually discover its full potential for themselves.

For your own benefit, read every network marketing and self-improvement book that you can get your hands on. The many different approaches you will read about will widen your experience and add greatly to your knowledge of the business, and hence to your income possibilities.

While reading, always bear one thing in mind – there is nothing like experience. I have known quite a few 'readers' in my time, who pounce on every book that they see, but lack the ability to actually get out there in the field and do the business. They are readers, not doers. They spend each night reading, when they should be working.

I'm quite sure that readers of this book will not fall into the same trap.

Will you?

Whatever your favourite medium, do not ignore the others. Versatility is one of the keys to success. Use every possible method available to recruit. Your mind should be working every waking moment on new ways to get through to people. Become an innovator in your own right.

IN BRIEF

This chapter has shown you:

- **how to write letters with pulling power**

- **what not to write**

- **how to use mailing lists**

- **how to use video prospecting**

- **the use of audio-cassettes and books.**

NOTES, IDEAS AND THINGS TO DO

– 10 –

THE BUSINESS STRUCTURE AND PLAN

Limited Liability

You will have to spend some time considering how you want to set up your business. It is worth taking a bit of time to look at the various options, because the way you set things up can seriously affect your tax position and your personal liability in case of business failure. Let's face it, some of the people who read this book are not going to do what it takes, or may get involved with a network marketing company that goes bust, leaving them unpaid, and they may end up with serious financial problems. This won't be you, of course.

As an alternative to running your business as a sole proprietor or in partnership, you can form your own limited company or buy one 'off the shelf'.

If you are registering a limited company – and I strongly recommend that you do so to protect your personal property in case of business failure – a search will have to be done, at your expense, to ensure that you are choosing a name that is unique. However, if you buy the company from a specialist agency the search fee will normally be included in the total package. If you buy a 'ready-made' company, which is the fastest way to get into business as a limited company, you will have to accept one of the names that the company supplies, but the names may already have been checked out.

As a director you pay tax on your income just like any employees you have, but you don't have to split all the profits between the directors. The extra profits can be kept in the company where they will be subject to corporation tax.

Bear in mind that if you are a director in a limited company and something goes wrong financially, you may only be liable for your holding in the company which can be very little, unless you have personally guaranteed any loans (which you should never do), but you will still be liable to be taxed as a private individual on your income. If, on the other hand, you are operating as a sole proprietor or in a partnership, you are (jointly) personally liable for any debts that you incur.

There are modest setting up fees if you form a company and you will have to submit your accounts annually for audit.

Your accountant will advise you on the finer details of the tax advantages and disadvantages. Remember, you are an independent distributor in your own right. You can choose whatever name you want for your company, provided it doesn't clash with someone else.

Don't choose a name that gives too much away. Instead, choose a professional, corporate-sounding name.

Partnerships

Many of the most successful distributors are husband and wife teams, but relationships can change over the years and even the most stable partnerships can and often do end in divorce, so be sure to have your solicitor draw up a partnership agreement for you. The law limits the number of business partners you may have to twenty. In the case of network marketing you would be better to recruit nineteen of them into the business as distributors rather than taking them all in as partners.

Another obvious snag with having a business partner is that you don't get to keep all of the profits yourself. On the plus side, your partner may vastly improve your business with his or her ideas, contacts and hard work. Two people who work well together can do far more than the sum total of the two working separately.

On the minus side, you may find yourself stuck with a partner who gradually loses interest and doesn't pull their weight. Unwanted partners can be very difficult and expensive to get rid of. If you do decide to part company with a partner, make sure that you have the partnership formally dissolved and that the public knows that it is no longer in existence, lest you be held liable for any debts run up by the partner. You can advertise that the partnership has ended and that you will no longer be held liable for your partner's debts, in a local paper or nationally if you have business outside your local area.

Tag partners

If you don't have a financial partner, it is a good idea to have a 'tag' partner. If you are familiar with wrestling you will know that a tag partner is the one who jumps in to rescue you or take over from you when you have been beaten up.

Two heads are always better than one, particularly in sales. If one person says something then the customer or prospect may suspect a lie. But if two people say it then they think it *has* to be true – as it should be. If people really want to find out if someone is telling them the truth they ask a second opinion. Then they are convinced.

Think how easy it is for your mind to be changed by consensus. If you are down in the dumps and you meet someone who says, 'You are looking great today', it makes you feel better doesn't it? Then, if someone else tells you that you look great, it reinforces the message and you start to feel great. All it took was two people to tell you the same thing and you believed it. If they had told you how terrible you looked then you would be looking for a doctor.

You can choose your best downline distributor to be your tag partner if your husband or wife is not teachable. By 'best' I don't necessarily mean the currently most successful, but the most enthusiastic, positive and long-term committed distributor in your group. You will have someone to plan with, to talk over your problems with, to bounce ideas off, to pick you up when you are down and to give you an incentive to get out on the road on a cold winter's night when you'd rather be sitting in front of a roaring fire. The bonus is that, unless you happen to be married or otherwise emotionally attached to your tag partner, if you fall out over something, it should not cost you a fortune to get rid of them.

If you are already attached you will have to agree to keep the relationship with your tag partner on a purely business basis, otherwise you may find that your close working relationship leads to naughty happenings and an increasingly complicated life.

The business plan

It is possible to start in network marketing without a business plan, but it is not advisable. Fortunately the company's marketing plan will have done most of the work for you, but that only tells what is possible, it doesn't tell what you personally will be attempting to achieve.

Normally a business plan covers at least the first year in business and preferably the first three years. It is an attempt to predict your turnover and profits during that period. Essentially, it can only be an educated guess at best, but with careful planning your guess can come pretty close to the mark.

A good business plan can be a very effective recruiting tool, as it can allow you to show your prospects what they could expect from the business. But there are a number of reasons for putting a business plan together.

If you are putting a plan together for the purposes of obtaining a bank loan, or other backing, you are going to have to err on the conservative side because the bank will periodically review your situation and you don't want to be constantly having to explain why you are failing to achieve monthly targets. If the plan is simply for your own benefit then you are going to find it very useful. You will be able to use it to keep track of your performance. When things go wrong you will be able to analyse your plan and find out why. Perhaps you will find that you are spending too much in a particular area and will thus be able to change that and gain more profit. Perhaps you will find that one line is out-performing all the others, so you will know that you should concentrate on that line.

Most start-up companies fail within their first year simply because of poor bookkeeping. If they had kept track of things properly, on the type of business plan that is described here, they would have seen their problems coming and been able to take action to save things.

The plan should cover the following areas.

Decision basis

Why have you decided to embark upon this particular business? Give details of the reasons that led up to your decision.

Market research

Have you proved that the products will sell? The company's track record should help in this area.

Details of the competition now and anticipated in the future. If your company has only one product line, your business could be ruined by a cheaper or better competitor coming on to the market, but bear in mind the first principle of direct sales – whoever gets there first usually get the sale.

Capital available

Especially if you are starting out on a full-time basis you will normally be expected to contribute at least a proportion – perhaps 20 per cent of the start-up costs and to have enough capital to live on until your business starts paying off. One point is worth repeating here – never personally guarantee loans.

A lifelong friend of mine, whose business was destroyed by a single piece of paper that he never obtained – planning permission – made the mistake of personally guaranteeing business loans. He is now living in a tiny house in a high crime area as a result of the bank foreclosing on his impressive residence.

If you can't obtain the money you need without a personal guarantee, revise your plans. Be more patient. Start smaller and prove that you can earn the money before you go pushing vast sums into the business.

Another way to raise the cash is to seek out business partners who will invest, but you will have to give them a good return on their investment.

Yet another way to proceed is to sell your product only wholesale, to new distributors whom you have personally recruited, and to demand payment in advance. It is a difficult way to proceed, but there are a number of network marketeers who have been very successful in this way. Once you have someone

hooked they are so keen to get their hands on stock that getting
the money up front is not usually a problem.

Start-up costs

There are many ways of starting and many levels of start-up costs.
Work out the cost of your initial stock and office setting up costs,
taking everything into consideration. Are you going to be working
from home or will you open an office in town? Remember that all
you really need to start is some product. You can then go out and
sell it. With the income thus produced you can buy some more
product and go out and sell it, gradually building up both your
stock and a team. Some of the most successful distributors in the
business have started like that.

If you do decide to open an office, will you be employing staff?
It is best to delay taking on employed staff until you have a big
enough business to justify the expense, but perhaps you can afford
to start in a big way right from the word go.

Do you need centre of town premises or will a less central office do?

Office equipment

You will need a telephone, preferably with a combined fax/
answering machine. You will find a computer with word process-
ing, an accounts program and a mail merge program very useful.
Also useful – all sorts of miscellaneous office equipment such as
photocopier, paper, headed notepaper, business cards, phone
books, wall planner, desk diary, calculator, account book, cash
box, filing cabinet, desk and chairs etc. The equipment level that
you go for is entirely your own choice. If you are really good at
economising you will be able to get much of it second-hand. You
may also be able to get a grant and a low interest loan from a city
development company to help with your start-up costs. In certain
areas you could get a rent-free period of up to a year.

Additional office costs and benefits

Additional costs may include business rates, preparation costs of
conforming to fire regulations and special planning regulations,

other preparation of premises including fittings, painting, and decorating and heating. If you are moving into an old premises get a reliable builder or surveyor to look it over. It may need a lot of hidden work like rewiring or timber repairs and preservation.

If you choose to work from your home the most important point to consider is space and light. You will need somewhere to work where you will not be interrupted by the normal household routine. It is no use trying to make phone calls with screaming kids or a vacuum cleaner buzzing in the background. It is also no use trying to cram all your things into a linen cupboard. If you have a box room or an attic that you can convert then that is ideal. Failing that, you can reorganise your bedroom. You could even convert your garage or garden shed.

You will still require many of the same items that you would need for a proper office, but you will save a small fortune on things like rent, rates, additional phone connection and electricity. On the other hand, if you had an office in town it would add considerably to your status, and you could perhaps retail some of your product from it and make additional profit by selling office equipment and stationery, or whatever best ties in with the sort of products that your company deals in. But never forget that the sort of products sold through network marketing do not tend to sell well off the shelf and no matter how much passing custom you get in town, you will never equal the turnover of a successful network marketing organisation.

Advertising

How did you find out about your network marketing company? Was it through advertising? You can plan for the cost of an advertising campaign to get the ball rolling, but be careful. If you break the company's rules in this area they may suspend you or even remove you from their computer and thus put you out of business until you find another company with suitable products. So, before you go out and start planning what you are going to say in your adverts, find out what you are permitted to say by your network marketing company. You may find that the company publishes a list of permitted adverts. You may even find that the company does not permit any adverts at all.

You will also have to conform to the Trade Descriptions Act, which makes it illegal to describe goods, services or prices falsely.

Shop window adverts

To help you build a team of small distributors you may find that shop window adverts work very well. It is a good idea to carry a number of pre-prepared adverts and whenever you spot a shop with ads in the window, stop and put one in. While you are at it you can have a look at who else is advertising in the shop. You can take down the numbers of anyone who is advertising for work and invite them to meet you for a coffee. You can say something like, 'I happened to notice that you are advertising your services in the local shop. I am actually looking for someone who is interested in making a bit of extra money. How would you like to meet me for a coffee and we will see if we can help each other out?'

Bear in mind that many people doing one or two sales a week will make you far more than one or two team members doing a lot. Don't ignore the little distributors. They will make up 90 per cent of your business and make you most of your income.

Maxim: **A lot of people doing a little will make you more than a few people doing a lot.**

Transport

I have spoken elsewhere of the value of a good car in terms of personal prestige. Now is the time when you will have to work out what you can afford. My advice in this matter is to get as good as you can afford. First impressions are so important that they can make or break you. If my sponsor had been driving a beaten up old car I would definitely not have been impressed, I would not be in this business and this book would never have been written. In fact, he was driving a brand-new executive BMW. I took one look at it, compared it to my rusty old heap and decided that I wanted one the same.

On the other hand, practical considerations must be taken into account. If your stock is particularly bulky, you may have to get hold of a van. If that is the case then make the best of it. Use the van as advertising space. Put up your network marketing company's logo and your own business name – you will probably have to use the words 'Independent distributor' to avoid giving the public the impression that you are an employee of the network marketing company that you are involved with.

Don't make the mistake of putting up product posters all over your van. People who see the van will judge your products from the posters instead of trying the items out for themselves.

Cash-flow forecast

This will be the best possible estimate of your anticipated income and expenditure over the planning period. From the analysis you should be able to work out your anticipated profits, but to get accurate results you will have to include absolutely everything. The forecast is done six months at a time, on a sheet of A3 paper divided into fifteen vertical columns with one column for headings, two columns for each month and two columns for totals. The first monthly column and totals column is for your estimates, the second is for your actual results. The sheet is also divided horizontally into two, with the top half for income and the bottom half for expenditure. By working out how much you can sell each month and your conservatively estimated percentage from your team of distributors, you should be able to work out the way your income should grow each month of your business.

The real income may differ considerably from your estimate. In the words of Robert Burns, 'The best laid schemes o' mice an' men gang aft a-gley', meaning that very little turns out in life exactly as we plan it. What we really hope, of course, is that the real income will be much higher than your conservative estimate, but only you can control that. The rewards in network marketing depend almost entirely on the effort that you put in. Being willing to do it is one thing. Doing it is another. It is not what you say you will do, it is what you do do that counts.

Keeping Accounts

If you have never been in business for yourself before, you may think account keeping is a very complicated business. Have no fear, it can be simplified. All you really need is a standard self-employed accounts book which you should be able to purchase from any good supplier.

The basic principle is that you keep track of all your income, which goes into a separate column for cash or cheques and all your expenditure which goes into separate columns for your main outlays like transport, stock, stationery, telephone, rates, training, miscellaneous. In this way, you can easily bring monthly totals for each item to use on your business plan.

Computer accounts programs are based on a very similar principle to account books, except that they do the calculations for you. Before getting one, buy lots of magazines for your particular computer and read about the different packages that are available. It is a fact that most people use only a fraction of their computer's capabilities, so don't go overboard with an expensive program that you will never need. If you do so, you may be one of the many computer-assisted failures in business. A second-hand machine can often do almost as much as a top of the range brand-new model costing ten times as much. It just does it a bit slower.

IN BRIEF

This chapter has shown you:

- **the advantages of limited liability**
- **how to choose a company name**
- **how to work with partners**
- **how to put together a business plan**
- **how to set up your office**
- **how to advertise**
- **cash-flow forecasting**
- **how to keep accounts**
- **your income tax liabilities.**

You have also been warned never to guarantee loans.

PROFESSIONAL NETWORK MARKETING

NOTES, IDEAS AND THINGS TO DO

– 11 –

THE CHICKEN LIST

So far you have been working with the 100 or 200 names on your prospect list. How honest have you been with yourself? It is now time to put down the names of all those people that you are afraid to approach. You know – the chairman of that board of directors, the president of that company, that doctor you know, the dean of your son's college, that lawyer, that politician. The more influential they are the better. It is surprising how many high-ranking professionals are dissatisfied with their lot. They are probably making a good income, so long as they continue to do what they are doing, but how much free time do they have? One of the benefits that almost everyone in conventional business really envies about network marketing is the amount of free time that successful distributors have available.

The pension scheme

Another of the benefits that interests professionals is the network marketer's built-in pension: repeat sales and perpetual network expansion. When a successful distributor retires in this business after perhaps three to five years' hard work if they so choose, they are not reduced to half pay or less as in most other businesses. In fact, if they have chosen their company carefully, their income will continue to grow regardless of the fact that they are no longer active. When a tree puts down good roots, deep into the ground, it has become independent of the gardener who planted it. In a similar way our network continues to grow after we retire. In fact, the network will grow even after we are dead, another plus point in our favour. This business is an asset that is inherited upon your death just like all your other assets. You can write a will splitting the future income between your wife and your dependent children or dispose of it in any other way that you choose.

A close friend of mine, who started at the very bottom of the ladder of network marketing, built up a substantial business by outstanding personal sales and by sponsoring. He died in a helicopter crash on his way to a training session where I was waiting for him. His death was a real shock. He was full of vitality and still young. At his funeral his wife was devastated. She told me that he had no insurance. 'We kept putting it off,' she sobbed.

I can still remember the relief on her face when I told her that his downline was strong enough to survive and provide an income for her that would grow indefinitely. At the time of writing his estate is now worth double what it was then and it is still growing.

Wealthy prospects

Perhaps your top prospects are already very wealthy. That doesn't rule them out. Having a viable network marketing business is far better than having a large amount of capital. You can spend the capital and be left with nothing. It can be badly managed or lost in some stock market crash, or stolen from some pension fund, but with network marketing, even when you spend or lose every penny that you have, you know that another cheque is coming in at the end of the month. How many successful businesspeople do you know who would like a guaranteed income for life for themselves, for their children, for their grandchildren and beyond?

I know of one man who has pulled ten millionaires into our business. What do you think brought them in? A number of them were asked this question and they all gave the same answer, 'The incredible long-term potential.'

The approach

The way in which you approach your top prospects is very important. I have found that you must allow them to discover the business for themselves. The higher up the corporate, social or financial ladder people are, the more sceptical they are likely to be about network marketing, especially if the business has been suggested to them by someone on a lower rung of the ladder of life. But, if they discover it for themselves, they see the business in a wholly different light. It is something new that they, with their unique eye for a business opportunity, have spotted while lesser individuals have missed their chance.

Ask for their advice, but insert facts in your questions that will make them curious. Start with flattery:

> 'I have approached you because you are about the most successful person that I know. I'm investigating a marketing business that I've been told has incredible long-term potential and I do know that many of the top people involved are taking twenty weeks' holiday and making over a million a year, but I'd really like your help in evaluating the company to make sure that everything is above board. Do you have the contacts to check something like this out?'

If you have chosen your network marketing company wisely and if the prospect agrees to help you – and in my experience most people will agree – they will gradually become intrigued with the business concepts and the long-term potential. They will ask you for the research that you have done so far and you will have to be able to provide it – but don't give them too much.

You may think that this approach is slightly deceptive, but the truth is that since you never stop learning in this business, the results of the prospect's enquiries will be useful to you and you may be able to use the information. You should be forever investigating the potential of our business.

Now write down the names of eight top people to contact:

1. _____

2. _____

3. _____

4. _____

5. _____

6. _____

7. _____

8. _____

One-to-one

Before your first 'solo flight' with your new prospects, you should have watched your upline co-ordnating distributor doing a few one-on-one personal briefings. There is nothing to beat on-the-job training, so listen carefully to the chat that takes place. Your upline will be an expert of the one-on-one meeting so make sure that he or she helps train you. Practise with your wife or husband. You have to become totally confident with the presentation. Eventually the time will come when you have to do the same with your distributors.

Most prospects make up their mind about you within the first ten to twenty seconds of meeting you, so you have to make a good first impression. Remember the famous cliché, 'You never get a second chance to make a first impression'.

This is a business where your personal appearance of success counts for everything. A friend of mine has a very high success rate with high quality prospects which he attributes to his mobile phone. This is his technique – as his prospect approaches he is pacing backwards and forwards speaking on the phone. He waits until the prospect is in hearing distance and hurriedly finishes the call with a really good last line such as:

> 'Tell His Lordship that I am busy tonight, but I'll try and make it next week.'

> 'Hold the flight until I get there. It's imperative that I get there on time.'

> 'Send the Rolls to pick him up.'

'Hold until 12 tomorrow and sell 100,000.'

'It has to be a real Picasso.'

'We'll need a helicopter. See if you can get James and tell him to land at the usual place.'

The meeting

Smile warmly and shake your prospect's hand firmly. Don't hold on too long – that makes people uncomfortable. And do make sure that your hands are not sweaty.

You will probably be meeting in a hotel reception area or a lounge, so it will help if you have as compact a method of explaining the business as possible. The last thing you want is to have sheets of paper spread all over the table. You should be able to obtain a business presentation folder from any good stationers. You can fill its plastic pockets with the best company literature that you can find. You will also probably want to have a simplified explanation of the business on one or two sheets.

First of all, offer your prospect a cup of tea or coffee. Have a chat about the journey or the weather to put your prospect at ease. Don't be too formal, but do be businesslike. Don't jabber on about irrelevant matters. Do listen carefully to what your prospect says. People love good listeners. Have you ever been talking to someone who kept looking around, obviously not concentrating? Did that make you angry?

Here are the main points you should cover:

- How long the company has been operating.

- Position of the company in the marketplace. Market leader? Twenty per cent of the market share?

- Manufacturing and warehouse facilities.

- Company's growth rate over the last (say) three years.

- Number of direct employees in the company.

- Number of independent distributors in the company.

- Dun and Bradstreet rating – if any.

- Information about the products. Are they unique to your company?

- Details about the head office and company support.

- Structure of the business and brief details of the marketing plan.

- Income potential, short-term retail, long-term wholesale and organisation building.

- Show the prospect your latest monthly cheque or, if you have just started, a photocopy of your *upline's* monthly cheque.

The important thing to remember is that you are here to get advice from your prospect. Most people love to give advice and it is this little vanity that has got you the meeting with your prospect. Don't switch track now that you have got the prospect to the meeting. When you present each piece of information you should be asking the prospect for an opinion, e.g.:

'Do you think that 20 per cent of the market share after five years in business is a good performance in the particular marketplace that the company are competing in?'

'Do you consider that the manufacturing and warehousing facilities are adequate, bearing in mind the massive expansion that the company has planned over the next few years?'

'Would you be able to check this Dun and Bradstreet rating for me?'

And don't forget the most important question of all:

'What I'm really after is your honest opinion. I'd like you to help evaluate this company for me and let me know if you think it would be a good business to get involved with.'

Your prospect will ask you a lot of questions about how you got involved with the company, your personal contacts in the company, any 'inside' information that you have about the company, the management team, the company borrowings and investments and the long-term plans.

You need to be well prepared to answer them.

The company is the issue

Never make yourself the issue. You are not meeting to discuss yourself. You are meeting to discuss the company. You want your prospect to judge the company, which you know is already very successful, instead of you, who may not be so successful – yet.

Forbidden subjects

Never make any reference to religion, race or colour – even if you happen to know that you are in the same group as your prospect. These subjects have no relevance to our business. Never refer to another ethnic group in a derogatory way. You may hold beliefs which appear to be both wrong and shocking to your prospect. I have been very disappointed in some otherwise very intelligent individuals to find that they have common, crude prejudices which could be easily countered. I have found that it is a waste of time to argue with such people. Are you one of them? Such beliefs can only hold you back. In this business you have to love people to be successful. All people! If you don't yet then you have some personal development to take care of before you do anything else.

Find out about the prospect

Remember Dave Penney's maxim, 'People don't care how much you know until they know how much you care'? Think of this phrase whenever you are tempted to launch into a complicated explanation of our business. Stop yourself and ask your prospect the question, *'Tell me about yourself?'* The answer will always help you to fit the business to the prospect.

Never make the mistake of suggesting, on your first meeting, that your prospect might like to get involved with the company him or herself. This is the fatal mistake that is repeated time and time again, even by some fairly experienced distributors. It gives the lie to your whole meeting and your prospect will see through you, and possibly walk out on the spot. You will certainly never get another appointment with him or her.

The follow-up meeting

After your prospect has had time to investigate the company, arrange to meet again. Even then, if your prospect has come up with a favourable result, allow him or her to make the decision to get involved. If you have supplied the prospect with sufficient information and presented your facts without your opinions, and the prospect has that human weakness of most highly successful businesspeople – never passing up the chance to make money, then he or she may ask you how to get involved with the company. If not, don't push him or her.

Use the subtle approach. Let the prospect think on it for a while, then say that you have been invited to a business briefing and you would like him or her to come with you to help you evaluate it. The prospect's natural curiosity should have been aroused by this time so that he or she will be unable to resist the chance to find out more. Once you get the prospect to the briefing, the thought should occur that he or she could profit by getting personally involved instead of just acting as an adviser to you.

The punch line

If the prospect still doesn't put him or herself forward, after you have had a chance to discuss the briefing say that you have decided that you are going to get deeper involved yourself – in the light of the information he or she has helped you with. Ask if the prospect knows anyone who could be interested in getting involved with you, to help you with meetings, interviews and with profit planning.

The prospect may then put him or herself forward, or – since you can't win them all – he or she just may introduce someone else to you. With a personal reference, having thoroughly checked the company out, you should find the task easier this time.

IN BRIEF

This chapter has shown you:

- **network marketing's pension scheme**

- **the advantages for wealthy prospects**
- **the correct approach**
- **how to be one-to-one with top prospects**
- **the follow up**
- **the punch line.**

Notes, ideas and things to do

NOTES, IDEAS AND THINGS TO DO

NOTES, IDEAS AND THINGS TO DO

– 13 –

OVERCOMING FEAR

AND HAVING FUN

Fear of the unknown is one of the greatest hindrances to progress that exists. What kind of world would it be if there were no explorers?

I was watching my daughter's hamster the other night while she was cleaning out its cage – actually a redundant fishtank. Hamsters have a tendency to get lively when you have been handling them for a time and they become a bit of a handful, so I put it on a chair for a while and kept my eye on it. It ran from one end to the other looking for an escape, then it crept right up to the edge of the seat, and edged further and further over until it let go with its back feet and fell to the floor. Now, hamsters are very short-sighted and they have a very poor judgement of distance. The hamster had no way of knowing how far away the floor was, but it had the courage to make that leap in the dark. The urge to escape was stronger than its fear of the unknown. Would you have the same courage under the same circumstances?

There is always an element of the unknown when you start any business. You can plan for the future, but you can't predict it.

James Russell Lowell, the famous nineteenth-century author, poet and philosopher once said, in *Democracy and Addresses*, '. . . The misfortunes hardest to bear are those that never come.'

You have to take that leap into the dark to escape from your present circumstances. And when you are recruiting new distributors you need to look for people like yourself who will take that leap. Remember Butch Cassidy and the Sundance Kid when they leapt off the cliff into a river to escape from the posse? The river led them to new and greater adventures. I don't know if that

Notes, ideas and things to do

– 14 –

PROJECTING A SUCCESS IMAGE

The image that you project can determine your success or failure
in this business. Can you imagine the reaction of a stockbroker
turning up to a business briefing to find half the audience in T-shirt
and jeans. Would he or she come into the business? Or do you
think that you would project a good image if the meetings were
filled with studded leather-jacketed biker types? Not that there is
anything inherently wrong with bikers, but that is exactly my point
– people have filing-box imaginations and if you don't want to be
filed under 'layabout' or 'ordinary' then you have to look extra-
ordinarily successful.

If you want to attract the right sort of people into your business
then you need them to look at you not merely as equals, but with
admiration and envy. When you can make a merchant banker,
Lloyd's underwriter or a stockbroker feel that way then you will
be on the road to success. Don't think those negative thoughts –
that you could never achieve that image. This is a fun business, but
there is a serious side to it and no matter how professional the
briefing is, if the stockbroker does not feel in the company of
equals, then he or she is not going to feel at home.

Power Dressing

A friend of mine who is in the entertainment business was puzzled
at his lack of success with prospects. He came to me after a business briefing, having just lost another two and he asked for advice.

I took him over to stand in front of the full-length mirror in the
hotel lobby.

'What do you see?' I asked.

He looked puzzled. 'I see a successful businessman,' he said.

'I see a successful entertainer,' I said. He wore long hair, a light coloured suit, a brightly coloured shirt, numerous gold rings and, ridiculously, a gold medallion.

The following week his change of image brought him a standing ovation when he walked into the training room. He has never looked back since he realised the importance of separating his stage image from his business image.

To get the best possible reaction from high-quality prospects you should wear a modern styled dark grey suit with a white shirt or blouse and a brightly coloured tie (for a man). The tie helps to give that individual something that makes you stand out from the crowd. Black well-polished shoes and a leather briefcase add the final touches. Wear a company lapel badge if they are available. Ladies should, of course, always wear a bra unless the top you are wearing is supportive. Mild flirting is acceptable when business is finished, but you don't want your sexuality to distract your prospect when you are discussing business. In line with this sentiment, skirts should be fashionable but modest.

The handshake

Physical contact is very important. Don't be afraid to touch people. When you shake hands with someone, use a firm grasp with men but if you are unusually strong be careful not to hurt them. At the same time briefly grasp their forearm with your left hand. Think about it. Who has ever done that to you? The chances are that it was either a very close friend or an exceptionally confident individual who was probably at the very top of their profession. Don't be afraid. Do it. The air of confidence that it gives you is fantastic. It all adds to the image that you are putting across.

First impressions

To project an image of success, start from the beginning when you arrive at the hotel. What are you driving? If your car is a bit of an old banger then one of the first things you should do is get hold of a decent car. The more prestigious the better. It is very awkward always to have to park around the corner. I know, having done that for my first few months in the business. When I finally got a good car, the boost that it gave to my confidence was incredible. I could take prospects to my car to fetch brochures and product examples without making pathetic excuses like – 'My other car is in getting fixed'.

Put yourself in the position of a prospect awaiting a would-be sponsor. Imagine the scene. You are standing in front of a hotel and the person you are meeting drives up in a beaten-up old car which is backfiring and billowing smoke. The person gets out of the car with a red face and hunched shoulders, and launches into an apology. What would be your initial impression?

Now imagine this scene: You are standing in front of the same hotel and the person you are meeting drives up in a new, top of the range car. The person comes striding towards you confidently, head held high, and grasps you by the hand in a firm and confident grip. What would be your initial impression?

Which person would you feel most comfortable getting involved with in a new business venture?

I think we have established that projecting an image of success builds both your confidence and the confidence of your prospects. In order to project the correct image, you will have to work hard to get the 'tools' of that image. This helps you to keep your aims in focus. As you achieve each aim, from getting a new suit to purchasing a new car, you can tick them off your aims list. The satisfaction that this brings has to be felt to be understood.

You can't beat being neat

Men should be clean shaven. Beards are difficult to keep very trim and smart without looking ridiculous. Further, beards are often thought of as compensating for some kind of inadequacy.

Men's hair should be neat and trim, but not with that 'just cut' look. Women should keep their hair in good condition, and will probably wear it up or tied back if it is long.

Make-up or earrings are out of the question for men. For

7. _____

8. _____

9. _____

10. _____

IN BRIEF

This chapter has shown you:

- **power dressing**
- **the handshake**
- **first impressions**
- **neatness**
- **how to find the but factor**
- **how to understand body language.**

NOTES, IDEAS AND THINGS TO DO

NOTES, IDEAS AND THINGS TO DO

$-16-$

SNAGS AND OBSTACLES

Sod's law, which dictates that 'if something can go wrong, it will go wrong', seems to rule the network marketing business. You are going to have to cope with frustration worse than any you have ever known. Ever gnashed your teeth? Get ready to chew bricks!

Snag 1

People won't turn up when they say they will when you arrange to meet them.

If you can collect them, or arrange to have them collected, then do so. If you must arrange for them to make their own way then make sure that they know that you are going to a lot of trouble to get there and you will be waiting for them. Always phone to confirm meetings the day before. If you are travelling a long way then phone immediately before you leave just to make sure that they are still going. Even this won't make sure that they get there. It is surprising the number of prospects who seem to have car trouble on the way to meetings. I've had five people in a row claim that their car broke down on the same night.

Question: When does definitely mean probably not?

Answer: When you are discussing responses to invitations.

If someone says that they may come, then that means they won't. If they say they will probably come, then that means they probably won't. If they say they will certainly come, then that means they may come. If they say that they will definitely, absolutely, without question be there, then that means that there is about a one-in-three chance that they will be there.

I kept track of a hundred '*Absolutely-without-question-Rely-on-me-I-will-definitely-be-there*' confirmations. Thirty turned up. Of those that didn't:

Car trouble	27
Sudden illness	11
Changed mind	24
Forgot	6
Death	1
Broken ankle	1

A key phrase to remember is: 'I'll be waiting for you at reception.' Nobody actually likes to keep you standing waiting. It helps to appeal to their conscience.

Snag 2

Despite all your efforts, between 60 and 80 per cent of your hard-won distributors will drop out of the business within six months if the products are at all difficult to sell. They may learn how to do it, but they won't have that 'follow through' determination that it takes to make a success of the business.

As I mentioned earlier, these are no loss to you. You will have gained contacts from them and made profit from them. You just have to be philosophical about it and accept that the business still works despite the dropout rate. Those you are left with are the strongest and best distributors. This business favours Darwin's theory of natural selection. Only the strong (in spirit) survive.

Snag 3

People will fail to return your videos, audios and literature. Chase them up. You have paid good money for them. Keep track carefully of where every item is and never give up until it is returned. Here is one piece of advice. Never send your videos by post if you do not have a telephone contact number. It is too easy for people to ignore letters. If people keep on failing to return things after a number of telephone calls, try this approach:

> 'Hi Dave, John here. Listen – I need that video I sent you and I am going to be passing through your town at 2 a.m. next Friday morning on my way to London. I'll just stop by and pick it up, but don't bother to wait up for me. I'll bang on the door when I get there. Is that OK?'

Nobody is going to want you calling at 2 a.m. so they will usually post it to you. This method certainly works for me.

Snag 4

You will have to leave friends behind as you become more and more successful.

Relatives and friends will become jealous of your success. You can't please everybody. You will grow beyond certain people. They will see you moving into a bigger house, buying a bigger car, putting in a swimming pool, living an executive lifestyle and going on holidays. You are not going to have time to hang out at your local bar – you'll be too busy organising business lunches, training your ever-growing team and making new friends. The really good friends that you have – the tried and tested friends – will be delighted at your success.

You will make enemies. Jealousy is one of the great motivators. People will plot your downfall. People will deliberately try to frustrate you. They will talk behind your back, lie about you, try to steal from you and cheat you. On the last point there are crooks in network marketing, as there are in every business. They will not last long, but they can do a considerable amount of damage to the reputation of network marketing in general and to your business in particular during the time that they are involved. If you suspect that there are dishonest deals going on in your business, my advice is to weed out the culprits ruthlessly. Your loyalty is to your group and to the honest, hard-working distributors in it.

Snag 5

You will have to shoulder more responsibility.

A lot of people are going to be relying on you when you make it big. You will probably have some direct employees to cope with your mail and phone calls, as well as your downline to keep track of. You will have meetings to run, people to train, a timetable to keep to and an image to maintain. It is hard to be a hero, but a lot of people will be looking up to you.

Snag 6

People will say that you can't do it. They will say, 'It won't work here. You are going to be a failure. It's pyramid selling. Nobody can make that much money. Don't do it. You're mad!

Such people are the dream thieves. They may be disguised as your family or friends, but you have to see them for what they are. The only limit in network marketing is your imagination. If you can see it, you can be it.

Eventually, as your success becomes apparent, the dream thieves will change their tune and perhaps stretch to a few dreams of their own, but during the hard times, when you are fighting to make your business a success you are going to hear a lot of people saying,

> 'I told you this wouldn't work.
>
> I told you those things wouldn't sell.
>
> I told you network marketing was a con.'

There is only one answer to that. Put a smile on your face and say, 'Today has been a wonderful day and tomorrow is going to be even better!'

In truth, each day that passes is a day closer to your success, so you have a good reason to smile.

Snag 7

Lack of capital is a major snag that some distributors have to face. There are a number of ways round this. You could use your business plan to ask for a business loan, but don't forget that you should not have to commit any large amount of capital just to get started. Anyone who tells you otherwise is lying. As I've mentioned elsewhere, it is far better to prove that you can sell the goods before you commit to a large order and it's far better to teach your downline to sell before you accept a large order from them. You'll have the money clawed back if they fail.

Your income may take longer than you thought to build up to an acceptable level. This depends on your own efforts, but also on a certain amount of luck.

For example, it may take you longer to find the right people than you expected. You may find that you have to struggle financially for well over a year before you begin to rake in the benefits. No matter how tough the struggle, the long-term results will be worth it. To give up before you achieve success is the only way that you can lose in the end. Those who stick it out inevitably learn through their mistakes and achieve well-deserved success.

It is worth repeating that you should never give up your day job until you are certain that you are making enough on a regular basis to live on. Remember, a lot of that rebate cheque may have to be paid to downline distributors. Stick to your business plan and work out your true profit, taking all expenses into account.

Snag 8

You will have to work very hard for the first two to five years.

You may be used to taking life easy, working at your own pace, but that is all going to have to change. You'll be getting up early and working until late. You will have to give up your free time now, in order to gain more of it when you succeed. You will have to organise your day properly and use each moment to its fullest advantage.

The effort is worth it.

Snag 9

When you start to see the success happening you are going to be so excited that you will have trouble sleeping. You will wake up at 3 a.m. still thinking about the business. If you aren't then you should be!

Snag 10

The more money you make, the bigger your accountant's bill and the bigger your tax bill.

Perhaps the latter snag will not bother you so much as some of the others. Don't allow yourself to be flattered over some expensive free lunch into accepting biased investment advice.

Whatever happens, don't put all your eggs in one basket. Don't trust one person with all your money. Thousands of totally trusted accountants have disappeared to Brazil or Mexico with all their clients' money. Don't even trust one bank. Remember BCCI?

NOTES, IDEAS AND THINGS TO DO

Notes, IDEAS AND THINGS TO DO

– 17 –

MOTIVATING YOURSELF

Motivation, ambition, desire, drive, hunger, inspiration, interest, wish, impulse, incentive, incitement, inducement, instigation, reason, spur, stimulus.

You must have it or you wouldn't be reading this book, but how *much of it* do you have? Do you have the fighting spirit to battle against the odds or are you one of life's quitters, giving up in the middle of each enterprise before you have achieved anything?

Do you want to lie down and die or get up and live? **Motivation is what makes the difference between winners and losers**.

Most people would rather endure the hardships of having too little money rather than the hardships involved in earning a lot of money. **Both require the same energy expenditure.**

It is just as hard to struggle to survive on a subsistence income as it is to struggle your way to become one of the top money earners in the country. **Which would you rather do?**

To succeed in this business you have to decide not only what you want, but also what you are willing to give up. Keep doing what you are doing and you will keep earning what you are earning. You have to change to succeed.

Self-motivation is one of the essential keys to success in this business. It is not always easy to stay motivated. Inertia is perhaps the strongest enemy you will have to defeat. It is so easy to stay that extra hour in bed. It is so easy to put things off. It is very tempting to watch that film on the box or doze off in front of the fire.

You will find yourself thinking, 'What does it matter? I can always do extra tomorrow, I will feel more refreshed then.'

'I'll make a fresh start tomorrow.'

'Tomorrow I'll try harder.'

'I'll do it tomorrow.'

This is known as the *tomorrow syndrome*. What is wrong with the *tomorrow syndrome?* When tomorrow comes, there will be a new set of excuses for not doing the work, that's what!

Compare the *tomorrow syndrome* with what I call the *today syndrome*.

'Today I'm going to get out there and do it!'

'Today I'm going to be the best that I can be!'

'I'll do it now!'

Who do you think is most likely to succeed, someone afflicted with the *tomorrow syndrome* or someone motivated by the *today syndrome*?

Using the subconscious

The darkest time is just before the dawn. I remember a time when I was going through a particularly bad patch. I had been working desperately hard for months but hardly sold a thing. My wife was nagging at me to 'get a proper job'. Both my bank accounts were beyond their overdraft limit. The bank manager had refused to up the limit to allow me working capital. My car payment was over-due. I was behind with my mortgage. I owed money left, right and centre to local firms. My electricity and phone were on the point of being cut off. I sat slumped with my head in my hands, on the point of despair. I had explored every avenue to try and ease my situation, but everything appeared to be closing in one me. I had begun to think the darkest of all thoughts – that I was worth more to my family dead than I was alive and, worse still, that network

Pessimist: I've written off my car. What a disaster.
Optimist: I've written off my car. Great. Now I'll get a better one.

Pessimist: My partner has left me and now I'm all alone.
Optimist: My partner has left me. Freedom at last.

Pessimist: My purse is half empty.
Optimist: My purse is half full.

I remember as an eighteen-year-old in the army I was giving a sergeant a hand with building an extension to the sergeants' mess. He was a bricklayer by trade and liked to keep his hand in. Unusually for him he was in a bad mood. Anyway, we were just about finished for the day when he told me to throw up a brush to wipe off the cement joints. Well I couldn't do anything right that day. He was about 12 feet up and I threw the brush too hard, so he had to move suddenly to try and catch it. He stepped on the wrong end of a scaffolding plank and it stood on end, letting him fall down the gap. To make matters worse he dragged down some of the freshly built wall on top of him. On the way down he gave a sort of ragged, intermittent cry as he bumped and scraped off the rest of the scaffolding.

For a second he lay in a twisted heap and I froze in shock, but then he groaned and I ran over to help him. I'm ashamed to say that I was more worried about what he was going to do to me, than I was about what had happened to him.

After pulling the timber and bricks off him, I grabbed him under the armpits and dragged him into the open. He was still groaning, but recovering fast. I told him to stay still until I got help, but he would hear none of it. He sat up and peeled up his trouser leg to reveal a very badly scraped shin.

'That was lucky,' he said, 'I could have broken my leg.'

He seemed to have forgotten my part in his downfall so I kept my mouth shut. He got up and hobbled along a few steps and then stopped, gazing up at the platform.

'In fact,' he said, 'if you look up at that scaffold, I could have hit that bar with my chin on the way down and broken my neck.'

He grinned at me, all trace of his previous ill temper gone.

'This is my lucky day,' he said. 'It's when something like this happens that you realise that it's great to be alive!'

The sergeant was a natural optimist. His good-humoured outlook made everybody like him and made his life a lot easier. Sergeants do have authority, but if a soldier doesn't want to do something then he generally finds a way to avoid it.

A positive attitude will draw people to you. If you have that then you can hardly fail, but there is one other thing that you need and that is persistence.

Persistence

Of all the qualities that you will find in the most successful people from every walk of life, the one that crops up without fail is persistence. If you have it in abundance it makes up for a lot of failings in other areas. If you lack persistence, no matter how intelligent you are, no matter how well organised you are, no matter how good a salesperson you are, you will never succeed.

Until you have decided that no matter what happens, you will never give up, you haven't given this business enough commitment to succeed! It doesn't matter if you have done fifty presentations and never made a sale. What do you do then, call yourself a failure and give up? Don't be such a loser. One of the most successful distributors I know made over 2,000 demonstrations without a sale when pioneering his company's product breakthrough into the market. Most ordinary people would have given up long before that 2,000th 'No' and changed companies or turned to some other type of work. Here is where the power of his persistence came into its own. Instead of giving up, he reassessed his methods, decided that he needed training and ended up starting over again with his new knowledge. Less than two years later he had built a massive international organisation and was – and still is – generating a strong six-figure income and having more fun than any other ten men I know into the bargain. The best part of it is that he did all this with those same products that he got 2,000 negative results with.

3. _____

4. _____

5. _____

6. _____

7. _____

8. _____

9. _____

10. _____

IN BRIEF

This chapter has shown you:

- **the importance of self-motivation**
- **how to listen to that inner voice**
- **how to boost the self-image**
- **the value of optimism**
- **the importance of persistence above all**
- **the mountain and why you need to climb it.**

NOTES, IDEAS AND THINGS TO DO

NOTES, IDEAS AND THINGS TO DO

– 19 –

BUDGETING YOUR

TIME

Use it or lose it, that is time. It is the most valuable asset that you have, yet you spend it freely without thinking. Each moment of it that you waste is an opportunity never to be recaptured. If you want to achieve your purpose in buying this book then I suggest that you start to budget your time in the same way that prudent housekeepers budget their income.

Start with a daily budget. Work out how much you can afford to spend on each item. Figure out what you really have to spend. Cut out the luxuries. Try to save something each day.

Daily plan

Rise early. One of the most successful distributors I know, an ex-fisherman, built his business by actually being out on the road at 6 a.m., visiting fish markets, talking to fishermen and market workers, and making appointments for home visits in the evening. He puts his success down to hard work and honesty. After a year in network marketing he was earning more in a month than most people earn in a year. Do you want to emulate his success? Then emulate his hard work.

Get a really good desk diary. Each night before you go to bed review how your day has gone and write it up in your diary before planning your schedule in detail for the next day. Set yourself daily targets, depending on the income you require from the business, and go for them with every ounce of commitment you possess. If you decide to write five letters per day, make five phone

Week No.	Contacts made	Videos	Demos	Sales	Distributors signed
Mon					
Tues					
Wed					
Thur					
Fri					
Sat					
Sun					

As a precaution against them trying to deceive you, get them to send you a weekly list of the phone numbers of their new contacts.

Planning for success

One of the most important items of equipment that you can have is a good desk diary/planner. This will give you an overview of the whole month or even the whole year. You will be able to see at a glance when your appointments are, what you have planned, when your trainings are and when your holidays are.

Blanks? no thanks!

The gaps that you see in your schedule are also important. They are there to be filled. My grandfather, who was Lord Provost of his town and always had a very full schedule, told me the story of a postmaster-general who was asked in March to speak at a function to be held at the end of August. He had to turn the invitation down because his diary was already full for that month. Such good planning was the very reason for his success. If you can emulate the postmaster then you are sure to make a success of your business.

A major reason for failure in many sales businesses is lack of planning enough future appointments to give the high turnover necessary for success. If you get up in the morning and look at your diary only to find a blank page, then what are you going to do? Muddle through? The chances are that you will fiddle around and make excuses for doing nothing. You may make some phone calls, sort out some mail and justify yourself by saying, 'Well I needed a rest anyway.'

The trouble with failing to plan is that you will inevitably find yourself with far too much time to relax. It is unlikely that you will make money while messing about at home, though at sports and leisure clubs you can make contacts who can help you make money. The general rule is that if you begin to think that the business is great because you get so much free time, then you are definitely not going to make it in a big way. You should only get free time if you build it into your schedule. Success doesn't come easily in any business. It is a sore fight.

The further ahead you can plan, the more successful you will be. Plan months ahead if you can, but be flexible and get your priorities right. Concentrate on money-earning activities. Everything else has to fit in around that. For every working day in your diary break each hour into three and fill each twenty-minute slot with something to do, or with a business appointment.

Here is a typical successful network marketing distributor's diary page for one day. You may be shocked at how full it is. You are going to have to get used to the idea of working very hard if you want to fulfil your purpose in getting this book.

Maxim: **Keep your diary full to keep your bankbook full.**

A Typical Diary Time Budgeting Page

6.30 Listen to motivational tape while eating breakfast. RSVP aims.

7.00 Write letters.

7.20 Ditto.

7.40   Check and organise stock. Go over daily, weekly and monthly plan, changing schedules according to importance.

8.00   Sort out list of phone calls to be made today.

8.20   Leave for first appointment.

8.40   Meet JM for working breakfast.

9.00   Meet group members for short brainstorming session.

9.20   Three-way phone call with JR and HH. Start day's other calls.

9.40   Complete phone calls.

10.00   Coffee. RSVP aims.

10.20   Meet JK (check office for messages).

10.40   Meet LD (take samples).

11.00   Meet KM (introduce to Mary D).

11.20   Business evaluation meeting. (Rehearse product slot.)

11.40   Ditto.

12.00   Meet with BC to arrange adverts.

12.40   Check with office for messages and mail.

1.00   Working lunch with group. (Get Sam motivated.)

1.20   Ditto. (Progress report from all present.)

1.40   Sales calls. (Refer to dedicated sales schedule.)

2.00   Ditto.

2.20   Ditto.

2.40   Ditto. (Check office for messages. Make sure stock order goes through.)

3.00   Meet RM at the Iron Horse.

3.20   Ditto.

3.40   Call JM ref. Europe and get copy of electoral roll for Jack's area.

4.00   Dentist. (RSVP aims while waiting.)

4.20   Ditto. (Write tips for this evening's meeting.)

4.40   Visit BB to close sale.

5.00   Call KW ref. chain purchase.

5.20   Help DD classify prospect list.

5.40   Check home for messages. Get showered and changed.

6.00   Evening meal.

6.20   Ditto.

6.40   Leave for meeting at Palace Hotel. Play motivational tapes.

8.00   Arrive at meeting. Make intros etc. (Make a point of collecting business cards from anyone new.)

8.20   Take direct sales slot. Use prepared tips.

9.00   Meeting finishes. Go for a snack with friends.

9.40   Head home. Listen to news on car radio. Play language tapes.

11.00   Arrive home. Kiss spouse. Check for messages and mail. Make sure tomorrow's schedule is organised totally. Write 1,000 words of marketing report.

12.30   Bed. RSVP aims. Late night, so set alarm for 7.30 instead of the usual 6.00.

A lot was packed into this day. You can see why this distributor is successful. How much of it do you think could have been achieved without planning?

Maxim: **Fail to plan and you plan to fail!**

Most important of all, don't let the thief of time steal away your future.

The thief of time

How many hours a day do you spend watching TV?

I don't care how addicted you are to your favourite programmes, you are going to have to give most of them up until you have made your fortune. Two hours every day is 730 hours a year. That is ninety-one working days of eight hours lost each year to you. Some people come in from their work and flop down in front of the TV for the rest of the evening – perhaps five or six hours per night. The same people may get up for the occasional look out of the window and see a new car parked across the road and say someting like, 'Look, there's that bloke across the road with another new car. How the hell does he do it?'

I'll tell you something. He doesn't do it sitting in front of the television watching very well-paid actors making money.

IN BRIEF

This chapter has shown you:

• **how to plan your day**

• **how to keep your 'family' tree**

- how to use action cards
- the value of a full diary
- a typical daily schedule
- who is the thief of time!

NOTES, IDEAS AND THINGS TO DO

NOTES, IDEAS AND THINGS TO DO

– 20 –

TRAINING DEVELOPMENT
AND BUSINESS BRIEFINGS

After some months' regular attendance at trainings, having learned the training slots and taken part as a teacher, there will come a point when you feel confident enough to start up your own trainings and business briefings in your chosen area. This is an essential part of your development and few distributors make it really big without taking this step.

Training

There are a number of options available. Some of the network marketing companies will subsidise trainings but some don't. You can form a training co-operative with other members of your group or even with other independent distributors who are not in your group.

When choosing a place to hold your trainings try to make as prestigious a choice as possible. It is not going to impress your potential new distributors if you hold your trainings in a disused scout hall. Choose a good hotel with good parking and a large reception area. Don't be afraid to bargain for the best rates. Remember that you will be bringing a lot of custom to the hotel, especially as your group gets bigger.

In return for your booking a regular slot for the next three or six months, the hotel should provide you with an overhead projector, a TV and video player, a flipchart and possibly a slide projector. The other training aids, such as videos, slides, transparencies and product, you will have to provide between yourself and your group or co-operative. There is a possibility that your network marketing company will help you with the loan of training materials, but don't count on it. They are more likely to offer to sell you the materials. This may seem selfish, but it is because of their low overheads that they can pass on so much of their profit to you.

Content

Network marketing training can be broken into three main subject areas: networking, sales and motivation. Each of these subjects has been covered in this book, but clearly any sales trainings that you set up will have to be directed towards your particular products.

As mentioned previously, you will be familiar with trainings by the time you get to this stage because you will have regularly attended trainings held by other successful distributors. You can emulate the best of them or you can develop your own.

Break each subject down into sub-headings and work with the top performers of your group to develop the training matter until you are satisfied that it is suitable for presentation.

Networking

- Prospecting (including telephone, letters and personal visits).

- Referrals (from sales and from prospects).

- Brainstorming techniques.

- Tailoring the business.

The sales call

- Product knowledge.

- Focusing in on the market.

- Product presentation.

- Sales psychology.

- Closing a sale.

- Incentives to buy.

- The competition.
- The value of the word 'No'.

Motivation

- Aim setting and revision.
- Personal development.
- Body language.
- Planning for success.
- Persistence.

For each sub-heading, you can introduce a different distributor to take the slot, with each slot lasting between ten and fifteen minutes. In this way you can gradually introduce your distributors to the responsibilities of taking trainings and working in front of an audience. There is the added advantage that the speakers will have to learn the particular subject they are taking. There is no better incentive to learning a subject than having to get up and speak in public about it. By swapping time slots around you can ensure that your whole group gets the chance to take each subject in turn.

When they get more experience you can hand over whole training sessions to your tag partner or another of the hardest working members of your group.

How much?

The fee you charge for training is entirely up to you. In most cases it is wise to charge just enough to break even after taking hotel fees and your guest speakers' expenses into account. You don't want your distributors to feel that they are being exploited. At the time of writing VAT is payable on training fees.

How long?

I would suggest that you hold half-day trainings weekly and whole day trainings once per month, but you have to decide what suits your group and prospects best.

Your company may have a training register that you can be put on to help attract people from other areas to your trainings. Don't be selfish about this matter. You are all in this business together. If you help other groups then you will be repaid tenfold in the help and co-operation that you will receive in return. Make as many friends as possible everywhere. Every training you go to is an opportunity to make new friends and, when you get right down to it, you are going to attract more people into this business because they like you, and therefore trust you, than for any other reason.

International trainings

If you hear of any international trainings or regional trainings being held then, no matter what it takes, get there yourself, and get your best prospects and group members to go with you. The psychological boost that you will get from seeing so many other successful distributors in one place, and listening to their stories, will push your motivation into top gear and sustain you through difficult times. Such is the power of top trainers to motivate. Such is the power that you will have to develop yourself. Record what is said and study it. Study their methods and gestures. Look at how they communicate and put a crowd at ease. That will be you one day! When you see the guest speakers at these events, take the opportunity to visualise yourself in their place. To be up there as one of the most successful distributors in your company has to be one of your aims. Unless it is, you will never achieve it.

Maxim: **You don't get what you don't try to get!**

Business briefings

In parallel with the trainings, you will be running business briefings. First, a few important points should be made.

Make sure that all invited are informed that they should wear business suits. Make sure that they arrive punctually by getting your distributors to pick up their guests. As previously mentioned, never rely on them to arrive on their own unless you enjoy disappointment.

When your distributors and guests arrive, give everyone name tags and have the guests introduced to the top earners at the venue – the ones who will be taking the briefing.

Don't let people meet in the bar. You need them sober to understand your presentation.

Get all your distributors and guests to register at a reception desk outside the briefing room. Don't charge guests a fee until they have enrolled as distributors, but charge distributors a fixed fee for each guest. Don't allow smoking in the briefing room. Ensure that mobile phones are switched off and that line telephones are unplugged. Make sure that everyone gets a good seat. Put someone on the door to prevent late arrivals from entering. If people arrive late, they miss important points and so can gain a false impression of the business. Worse still, they can have trouble finding a seat, they can throw a speaker off track and they can distract the attention of the audience.

Get the audience to participate by asking them questions, and get them to put their hands up or speak in response. Welcome old friends and ask new faces their names. Crack a joke or two before you start.

You have to 'work the audience' to animate them. There is nothing worse than a room full of long and unresponsive faces. In line with this sentiment, your link man or woman should be the person most comfortable with performing this task. It need not be you. You can hold auditions to find the best distributor for the task.

You can tell which of your distributors are keenest by which ones put themselves forward as volunteer speakers. Incidentally, these same distributors will be the ones who phone you at home to check on various aspects of the business. You shouldn't have to go chasing your distributors to make them work. If this is the case then you don't yet have the right people. It would be better to drop them and keep looking. If they are keen enough they will be chasing you. Only the chasers get to the top.

There are six main subject areas to be covered, within a forty-minute time slot.

- how to prepare
- a company profile
- network marketing's advantages
- the marketplace
- the product
- the opportunity
- the importance of testimonials.

NOTES, IDEAS AND THINGS TO DO

NOTES, IDEAS AND THINGS TO DO

$-21-$

WALK THE WALK

The 'walk the walk' principle is based around the f ct that when you act successful other people believe in you and you end up believing in yourself. Do you want to build a successful network marketing organisation? Then act as if you already have one. Learn the training and start taking slots yourself. Become totally confident, and think, act, walk and talk like a leader. Mix with the leaders of your organisation. You will learn a lot that can set you on the road to success.

This is taking positive thinking to the next logical step – positive action. Do you want to gain confidence? Then act as if you already have it. In the words of the song, 'Walk tall, walk straight and look the world right in the eye.'

When a young man joins the army you see the 'walk the walk' principle in action. From a slouching, long-haired layabout with no self-confidence and a poor self-image, he is transformed during his training into a smart, confident, professional soldier who can hold his head up anywhere. By acting the part, he becomes the part.

The same principle works in an actor who takes on a role and 'walks the walk and talks the talk' of a vicious murderer. When he goes home for the night he may find himself unconsciously thinking like his character part.

Do you want to be a good spouse or partner? Then act as if you are one. Take presents. Help them. Treat them kindly. By acting as if you are one, you become one.

I recently received a letter from a man who thanked me for that little piece of personal advice which he received at one of my trainings. 'It has changed my marriage and changed my life,' he wrote. That makes me feel good, but the advice is so simple. Common sense should tell everyone what to do, but sometimes people get into routines and habits that make them forget the most important and fundamental things in life. Unless you get your home life sorted out happily, it is unlikely that you will achieve the success you desire. Let's face it, happiness is more important than money. No one is truly successful if they are unhappy. What is the use of having a lot of money if you ruin your marriage in the process of getting it?

The other side of the coin is that those with a happy home life are more likely to make it big. It has been often quoted that behind every successful man is a good woman. I'd go further – behind every successful distributor is a happy partner in life.

Have you ever had to take charge of a panic situation? Here's how it's done: act like a leader. Take charge. Start telling people what to do and they will do it. It is as easy as that. Act like a leader and you automatically start to become a leader.

How to be a loser

Do you want to be a loser? Of course not, but act as if you are one and you will become one. Hang your head. Don't look people in the eye. Be over-apologetic. Display a total lack of confidence. Giggle nervously and crack bad jokes. Drink too much. Chain smoke. Dress shabbily. Tell everyone about your bad day and all the bad luck that you are having. Display dirty teeth and hair. Don't wash very often. Give up after the first few negative results. Waste each day shuffling paper or driving about. Don't keep proper accounts. Spend more than you earn. Hang about with other losers. Give a weak, floppy handshake. Waste all your energy in unprofitable pursuits. Spend each evening lying in front of the TV. Get up late. Never organise your time, so that when you do eventually get down to work you are running about like a headless chicken. Never take the advice of others. Walk the walk and talk the talk of a loser and, as surely as night follows day, a loser is what you will become.

I could go on. Does anyone really act like that? You'd better believe it. I see them every day wondering why success won't come. They think that they have done the right thing; they have joined a highly successful organisation, bought some stock and now they sit back waiting for the success that they were promised would follow. When it eventually dawns on them that it doesn't work like that, they go off on the search for another wonder opportunity that does offer money for nothing.

How to be a winner

Do you want to be a winner? If you didn't you wouldn't be reading this book. Act as if you are one. Hold up your head. Look people in the eye. Control every situation. Be likeable. Never lose your temper. Smile readily and help put people at their ease. Get rid of your bad habits. Look like a winner and act like a winner. Never waste your time or energy. Emulate other winners. Choose other winners as your friends and learn from them. Go out of your way to help others achieve success – not just the extra mile, but the extra hundred miles or whatever it takes – that is how winners in network marketing in particular, and in every other walk of life, achieve success.

Walk the walk and talk the talk of a winner, and you will become one.

Do you want to be a millionaire? Then act as if you already are one. Go to the right places. Meet the right people. Eat in the right restaurants. Mix with millionaires. Walk the walk and talk the talk of a millionaire. Join the right clubs – no matter what. You will make friends with great influence in the world of business. You may hear of deals that can make you a fortune. Most important of all, do what it takes to make the money. Remember, do what you are doing at the moment and you will stay what you are at the moment.

Do you want to be able to influence successful and important people? Then act as if you already *can* influence them. Offer them professional advice and you may find that they take it. Almost everybody who has ever succeeded in business has used this principle to some extent. No one is going to listen to a thing that you say, unless you have the appearance of a professional.

I have a friend who retired from the army as a warrant officer. For a number of reasons he decided that network marketing didn't suit him. For a while he was lost without the army regime and ended up packing shelves at a supermarket – a real 'come down' after being in charge of a company of men. But then he got hold of himself and decided to use the 'walk the walk' principle. He walked out of the supermarket, put on a business suit, got some business cards printed as an efficiency consultant, and started offering his services to factories and other businesses, working purely on a commission of the amount saved by the firm as a result of his recommended measures. With twenty-two years' experience of spotting slackers in the army he is able to earn himself a much larger income than the army was giving him. When he arrived at the first factory, with no way of knowing what was ahead of him, he walked the walk and talked the talk of an efficiency consultant. Because he had the courage to act the part, he now has the part.

Ooze money

Have you ever heard the phrase 'You have to have money to make money?' It's wrong! But you do have to look as if you have money.

Have you ever gone shopping when you didn't look your best, perhaps in clothes that were untidy? How did that make you feel?

Have you ever gone out when you knew that you looked great? How did that make you feel? Did you walk a bit taller than usual?

Imagine you are discussing the business with (say) a merchant banker that you have invited for a business lunch. Bear in mind that he will already be earning a serious five or six-figure income. Although good sense dictates that he shouldn't, the fact is that he will be judging you as much as he will be judging the business. It goes without saying that you will have to act and look really successful. In such a case it may even be worth hiring a Rolls-Royce just to let him see you getting in and out of it. It is hard to impress some people, but the harder it is, the harder you have to try.

If you want to impress a millionaire then look and act like a multi-millionaire. Go into the hotel or restaurant the day before your meeting and pay off the head waiter to make sure that they treat you like royalty. Get six people to come running when you snap your fingers. And then act casually as though this is the normal reaction to you. Always treat staff with politeness. Never get upset if everything doesn't go quite right. That would be a sign of petty-mindedness. True leaders never allow small matters to upset them. Generosity of spirit, friendliness to all and infectious happiness are the qualities that will make your prospect like you. If they don't like you, they will never join with you in a business venture. Would you?

Get noticed

The respect that comes to you in life is directly proportional to your appearance and your attitude. Other people notice your attitude and act accordingly, and that is really what this chapter is all about. Everyone, from hotel waiters to business partners and investors, will treat you the way you expect to be treated. Skulk into a hotel and stand in a corner waiting for someone to notice you, and it will be a long time before you are noticed. Don't be Mr or Ms Invisible, be unignorable. When it comes to the crunch, and you have to put your ideas across to your next potential new distributor, there is no hiding place. You will be judged more by your personal appearance, your confidence and your attitude, than by the potential of the business opportunity that you are offering.

When you walk into a room with your shoulders back, head held high and your confident stride, making eye contact with everyone, smiling at friends, dressed like a winner, well groomed, with your aura of confidence and energy, people will notice you. They will want to meet you. They will want a part of what you have and you will be richer in many ways.

The Ten club

There is an important principle here. When you begin to build your team there is a temptation to try to recruit those whom you can easily persuade. This usually means those who are on a slightly lower social scale to yourself. I believe that each and every one of us has equal value in society. The working person is the salt of the earth, and the ordinary person in the street has an intelligence, common sense, wisdom and humour that he is rarely credited with. But if you take people from the street into your business briefing, because it is easy to get them, then who will they bring? It is liable to be others like themselves or slightly lower on the social scale than themselves. And so it continues downhill until your business briefings are filled with the dregs of humanity pulled from downtown bars and street corners with the promise of a free drink afterwards. I have seen it happen.

The way to avoid this downhill problem is to go for those whom you regard as being slightly higher on the scale of life than yourself. At a recent seminar the audience were asked this question:

> 'Based on a scale of one to ten, with drop-outs and drug addicts as one, and real high-fliers and top achievers as ten, where do you see yourselves?'

The average answer was six. There were quite a lot of fives and sevens, a few fours and some eights. There was only one nine and no tens.

Now it is your turn. Where do you see yourself? Those of you who consider yourselves sixes should be recruiting sevens and eights. That is the principle.

Always aim up the social ladder. But if you still consider yourself a six, after reading this book, then you must be holding the book upside down. If you were a four before reading this book, you should now be a ten. If you were a five you should now be a ten. At the very least, you should now walk the walk and talk the talk of a ten. Soon, you will forget that poor self-image and you will be a genuine ten.

Join the Ten club now!

Maxim: Walk the walk and talk the talk of a winner.

Think big!

You may have to change the way that you are thinking in a radical way. Remember, 'Massive Action Brings Massive Results'. If you are used to small town deals and 'just getting by', and you want to change that to big city deals and 'making a fortune', then start thinking big.

Take a look at most of the successful distributors in your business. Find out what they are doing and just how successful they are. Do you want to be more successful than them? Then do more of what they are doing!

If you know a successful distributor who is writing five letters every day, speaking to five people every day, putting out five videos every day and inviting five people to a business briefing every day, then find out what he or she is earning.

Do you want to double that amount? Simply work twice as hard as that distributor. Put out ten videos every day. Invite ten people every day and talk to ten people about the business every day.

Do you want to triple or quadruple that distributor's earnings? Triple or quad the work level. In time, if you persist through the tough times, through the agonisingly slow start, through the disappointments, through the let-downs, through the broken appointments, through the Noes to the Yeses, and keep on doing it time after time after time, then and only then will success, double success, triple success and quadruple success come your way.

Saving

'You don't make a fortune all at once, you make it a bit at a time.'

If you have no money at all put aside then you are going to be for ever on the edge of desperation and so will find it difficult to 'walk the walk' with conviction. There is a simple, long-term solution to your problem, the 'tithe'. For many years it has been the custom in certain religions for those involved to give a tenth of their income to their church. Whether or not you are already doing this, it is a fairly small amount to put aside every week or month for personal savings. You may have to sacrifice something. You may have to economise in a number of ways, but when you start saving and thus start the accumulation of wealth you will gain in self-confidence and personal esteem.

During a training session, where I was invited to talk as one of the guest speakers, I mentioned the advantages of using the tithe system to put some money aside. Later I was approached by a gentleman whom I knew was a fairly successful distributor and was making a good income through his business. He drove an executive car, dressed in expensive clothes and wore a gold Rolex.

'I'll be honest with you,' he said. 'Things are not as rosy as they seem. I've never been very good at saving and at the moment I don't have a penny put aside to fall back on. It is really putting pressure on me, because I have a large mortgage, the car payments and a backlog of bills to pay. But when I heard your talk, it made sense and I'm going to give your system a try. I feel that I just may be able to make it work.'

'It's not my system, it's as old as the hills,' I said, as we shook hands. 'But let me know how you get on.'

About a year later he sent me a photocopy of his latest bank statement, which showed a substantial credit balance, with a note thanking me for bringing the tithe system to his attention. When I phoned him up for a chat he said that for the first time in his life he didn't have to worry about the size of his next cheque, and he was now a far more confident and relaxed person simply as a result of having some money behind him. Furthermore, he now makes all his distributors commit to saving a tenth of their income.

I was stopped in Edinburgh one afternoon by a lady who thanked me for her holiday. I was somewhat taken aback, since I could never remember seeing her before. She had attended a training session during my employment agency years.

'We didn't join,' she said, 'but I was at one of your trainings as a guest, and I heard you talking about saving up using the tithe system. Well, I thought it would work, and I tried it, and the result is that we have just had our first holiday ever. We went to Florida.'

That is the sort of result that makes everything worthwhile for me. Incidentally, I invited her back to attend a business briefing, and she is now a part-time distributor with a steadily growing little business.

One final word about saving. Let us picture a man aged about forty, who has worked about twenty years since leaving school. If he had saved one-tenth of his income during that period, he would now have approximately double his annual income put aside.

With wise investment he would be earning more in interest alone than many company pensions provide on retirement.

It may be too late for many of you to achieve the same by the time you are forty, but it is never too late to start.

This is the first day of the rest of your life.

IN BRIEF

This chapter has shown you:

● how to 'walk the walk' and 'talk the talk'

● how to be a winner

● how to ooze money

● how to join the Ten club

● how to think big

● the tithe system of wealth accumulation.

NOTES, IDEAS AND THINGS TO DO

NOTES, IDEAS AND THINGS TO DO

− 22 −

CONCLUSION

Network marketing has now reached such a degree of respectability that huge multinational corporations like Colgate Palmolive and Mastercard are using this fast and effective method of reaching the consumer.

For new companies, the first two years is the most risky period when inexperience and bad planning can cause failure.

For established network marketing companies, provided they are run properly and ethically, and keep introducing new product lines every eighteen months, or when their existing products have reached an optimum market share, there is no limit to the profit potential and the size of distributor groups operating. There has never been a product in history which has saturated the market. There has never been a network marketing company which has reached distributor saturation point. If there ever is, the company will be the most successful in history.

A warning

Hundreds of 'matrix' type companies which require substantial monthly investments are springing up overnight and offering massive automatic income for no work. All you have to do is keep investing and, in theory, as the matrix fills, you are pushed to the top and paid thousands. That is the theory, but I have yet to meet someone who has made a living from one of these schemes. I have, however, met a number of unfortunate individuals who have made heavy losses through matrix schemes. Many of the schemes are barely legal. Distributors patiently pay in thousands, sometimes over a period of years, waiting for the time when they will reach the top of the matrix and be paid out. Human nature provides the snag. They eventually lose patience or, because of a change in personal circumstances, can't keep up the payments.

The company wins and the individual loses! Unlike an insurance company, where the money invested would become a 'free paid up' policy, or could be cashed in minus expenses, or sold to an investment company, everything paid in is lost. The money you paid in has not been invested and held in your name. When you send a maxtrix company money, that money becomes the company's to do with what it will. And what it will do with it is usually spend it. Eventually you may get a letter saying that, unfortunately, no payout is forthcoming for the time being, because all investments have been eaten by 'expenses'. The company can change the rules whenever it suits them – and probably will.

Of course they are not all fraudulent, but do consider this – no company is going to give you money for nothing and anyone who says they will . . . won't. But please get in touch with me if you find a company that is genuinely giving away money. I'd like a piece of that action.

The levels

I haven't attempted to try and explain the many and various marketing plans and distributor levels. There are hundreds of companies and that would be an impossible task. There are some companies, having combined the best features of other existing plans, that prefer the name 'flexible marketing' to describe what they do. There are multi-level companies with a bewildering number of levels. There are many companies which pay only on 'levels' as compared to the more lucrative payment on 'generations'. Certain companies switch from levels to generations when you reach a qualification point.

Some companies have a multitude of little consumable products with a high repeat sale aspect and others have only a few high profit products that take from six months to three years for repeat business. Each system has its own merits.

There are numerous conventions as to distributor titles. Some companies use the various precious stones as badges of rank for their distributors, with the more precious indicating the higher levels. Others use names borrowed from conventional business such as 'area manager' or 'regional manager'. Some companies allow profit sharing and shareholding when you reach a certain level. Other companies reward you with a car and then make you work like hell to keep it, by forcing you to requalify each month.

As to training, there are companies that have been in operation for many years and yet have scarcely any training set up, while others have trainings in almost every city in the UK. If you are going for the top you will start your own.

Timing

There is no doubt that the most lucrative time to get involved with a company is during the initial market penetration period when you can set up your group to be ready for the growth period that always follows if the company has been successful, but it is during this initial period that the hardest work must be done. Once a product has achieved 10 per cent market penetration there is often a fast period of growth lasting between five and ten years. It is during this time that fortunes are made. The growth curve then tends to slow down considerably. You can thus make a lot of money with single product companies if you get in soon enough, but unless the product is something like insurance or a monthly magazine, sold the network way, with automatic repeat sales every month to subscribers, it is wiser to attach yourself to a company that is looking to long-term survival and growth by regular new product introductions.

Is it for you?

This business can be for everyone, but not everyone can be for this business. There are a few essential personality requirements which you will realise by now that you must have or be willing to develop.

You have to:

- get on with people;

- have character and personality;

- be willing to work hard;

- be flexible;

- have a good attitude;

- be ambitious;

- have stickability;

- be determined and persistent;

- have the deep desire to improve your situation.

And, most of all, you have to have **GUTS** – a genuine urge to succeed.

You will have made up your mind by now if network marketing is what you are looking for. To have got so far in this book you must have at least some of the above qualities. Now is the real test of your character. Start back again at the beginning and this time work through it properly, putting the advice to work immediately, taking notes and developing your own ideas as you go. Don't think you will waste the book by writing in it. The fact is that the book will be wasted if you don't.

If you do get involved in network marketing your life is going to change beyond all recognition over the next two to five years, provided you do the business properly and never, ever, ever, ever – through divorces, bereavements, famine, flood or war – under any circumstances, quit.

One final word. Really successful distributors have one thing in common: once they have found the right company with the right products, they stick to it through thick and thin. Changing companies is an admission of defeat. Winners never admit defeat.

Have fun.

Returned goods

The ongoing right to refund [minus handling] on returned goods will be restricted to within 30 days of receipt [for new participants].

Claw-backs

A company will be able to recover any payment from a participant only if the payment was made less than six months previously, and the recovery is in accordance with terms made clear in the participant's contract.

Limit on payments by new participants

The current limit of £75 within the first 7 days of joining will be increased.

VAT on goods returned

A promoter terminating a contract will have to pay the participant the VAT-inclusive price on goods bought-back.

Promotional material

The regulations will apply to any form of promotional material if:

- it is directed at potential participants;
- it indicates financial benefits from participation, and
- it is not subject to the Advertising Standards Authority's codes.

It is likely that all promotional material of more than 10 words will have to include:

1. the name and *address of the promoter;
2. a description of whatever is sold through the scheme.

* The government are considering making the requirement for the promoter's address apply only to material of more than 100 words.

Anyone wishing to be sent a copy of the revised draft regulations when they become available should write to:

Consumer Affairs 2b
Department of Trade and Industry 4.G.19
1 Victoria Street
London SW1H 0ET

USEFUL NAMES AND ADDRESSES

Direct Selling Association, 29 Floral Street, London WC2 9DP

British Standards Institution, 2 Park Street, London W1A 2BS

Department of Trade and Industry, 123 Victoria Street, London SW1E 6RB

Advertising Standards Authority, Brook House, 2–10 Torrington Place, London WC1E 7HN

The Design Council, 28 Haymarket, London SW1Y 4SU

Patent Office, Cardiff Road, Newport, Gwent NP9 1RH

Office of Fair Trading, Field House, Breams Buildings, London EC4A 1PR

National Economic Development Office, Millbank Tower, Millbank, London SW1P 4QX

The Company Store Limited, International Company Formation Agents, Harrington Chambers, 26 North John Street, Liverpool L2 9RU

Companies House, Crown Way, Cardiff CF4 3UZ (For England and Wales)

Companies House, 100–2 George Street, Edinburgh EH2 3DJ (For Scotland)

INDEX

PIATKUS BUSINESS BOOKS

Piatkus Business Books have been created for people who need expert knowledge readily available in clear and easy-to-follow format. All the books are written by specialists in their field. They will help you improve your skills quickly and effortlessly in the workplace and on a personal level.
Titles include:

General Management and Business Skills
Be Your Own PR Expert: the complete guide to publicity and public relations Bill Penn
Complete Conference Organiser's Handbook, The Robin O'Connor
Complete Time Management System, The Christian H Godefroy and John Clark
Confident Decision Making J Edward Russo and Paul J H Schoemaker
Energy Factor, The: how to motivate your workforce Art McNeil
Firing On All Cylinders: the quality management system for high-powered corporate performance Jim Clemmer with Barry Sheehy
How to Collect the Money You Are Owed Malcolm Bird
How to Implement Change In Your Company John Spencer and Adrian Pruss
Influential Manager, The: how to develop a powerful management style Lee Bryce
Leadership Skills for Every Manager Jim Clemmer and Art McNeil
Lure the Tiger Out of the Mountains: timeless tactics from the East for today's successful manager Gao Yuan
Managing Your Team John Spencer and Adrian Pruss
Outstanding Negotiator, The Christian H Godefroy and Luis Robert
Problem Solving Techniques That Really Work Malcolm Bird
Seven Cultures of Capitalism, The: value systems for creating wealth in Britain, the United States, Germany, France, Japan, Sweden and the Netherlands Charles Hampden-Turner and Fons Trompenaars
Smart Questions for Successful Managers Dorothy Leeds

Personnel and People Skills
Best Person for the Job, The Malcolm Bird
Dealing with Difficult People Roberta Cava
Problem Employees, how to improve their behaviour and their performance Peter Wylie and Mardy Grothe
Psychological Testing for Managers Dr Stephanie Jones

263

Financial Planning
Better Money Management Marie Jennings
How to Choose Stockmarket Winners Raymond Caley
Perfectly Legal Tax Loopholes Stephen Courtney

Small Business
How to Run a Part-Time Business Barrie Hawkins
Making Money From Your Home Hazel Evans
Profit Through the Post: How to set up and run a successful mail order business Alison Cork

Motivational
Play to Your Strengths Donald O Clifton and Paula Nelson
Super Success Philip Holden

Self-Improvement
10-Minute Time And Stress Management Dr David Lewis
Creative Thinking Michael LeBoeuf
Napoleon Hill's Keys To Success Matthew Sartwell (ed.)
Organise Yourself Ronni Eisenberg with Kate Kelly
Quantum Learning: unleash the genius within you Bobbi DePorter with Mike Hernacki
Right Brain Manager, The: how to use the power of your mind to achieve personal and professional success Dr Harry Alder
Three Minute Meditator, The David Harp with Nina Feldman

Sales and Customer Services
Art of the Hard Sell, The Robert L Shook
Commonsense Marketing For Non-Marketers Alison Baverstock
Guerrilla Marketing Excellence Jay Conrad Levinson
Guerrilla Marketing Jay Conrad Levinson
Guerrilla Marketing On The Internet Jay Conrad Levinson
How to Win Customers and Keep Them for Life Michael LeBoeuf
Sales Power: the Silva mind method for sales professionals José Silva and Ed Bernd Jr
Selling Edge, The Patrick Forsyth
Telephone Selling Techniques That Really Work Bill Good
Winning New Business: a practical guide to successful sales presentations Dr David Lewis

Presentation and Communication
Better Business Writing Maryann V Piotrowski
Confident Conversation Dr Lillian Glass
Confident Speaking: how to communicate effectively using the Power Talk System Christian H Godefroy and Stephanie Barrat

He Says, She Says: closing the communication gap between the sexes Dr
    Lillian Glass
Personal Power Philippa Davies
Powerspeak: the complete guide to public speaking and presentation
    Dorothy Leeds
Presenting Yourself: a personal image guide for men Mary Spillane
Presenting Yourself: a personal image guide for women Mary Spillane
Say What You Mean and Get What You Want George R. Walther
Your Total Image Philippa Davies

Careers and Training
How to Find the Perfect Job Tom Jackson
Jobs For The Over 50s Linda Greenbury
Marketing Yourself: how to sell yourself and get the jobs you've always
    wanted Dorothy Leeds
Networking and Mentoring: a woman's guide Dr Lily M Segerman-Peck
Perfect CV, The Tom Jackson
Perfect Job Search Strategies Tom Jackson
Secrets of Successful Interviews Dorothy Leeds
10-Day MBA, The Steven Silbiger
Ten Steps To The Top Marie Jennings
Which Way Now? – how to plan and develop a successful career Bridget
    Wright

**For a free brochure with further information on our range of business titles,
please write to:**

**Piatkus Books
Freepost 7 (WD 4505)
London W1E 4EZ**

PIATKUS

About the Author

John Bremner is an independent network marketing consultant and trainer. Everything he writes is based on his personal experience. He has learned his lessons the hard way, and thus knows how to help others to avoid mistakes and go on to achieve their own success. His working methods and ideas are used by many top distributors, and he has regular tutorial columns on network marketing in a number of business magazines, and is also published on the Internet. Additionally, he has produced an interactive *Network Marketing Masterclass* containing over 20 individual lessons, available on PC disc. (Windows™ 3.1 or later required.) Call (+ international code if outside UK) 01847–895918 for details of how to obtain this.